THE BIGFOOT ALIEN CONNECTION REVISITED

RONALD C. MEYER

MARK REEDER

HANGAR 1 PUBLISHING

PRAISE FOR THE BIGFOOT ALIEN CONNECTION REVISITED

The Bigfoot Alien Connection Revisited is an important step in moving away from the materialist mindset that Bigfoot is a physical being interacting with humanity. The research of the many Ph.D. academics of the Consciousness & Contact Research Institute, or CCRI, supports the thesis of this book that Bigfoot might be a consciousness-based inter-dimensional phenomenon, similar to the other paranormal Contact Modalities. This is an important paradigm shift in Bigfoot research, and I highly recommend the book.

Rey Hernandez
Director, Consciousness and Contact Research Institute (CCRI)

Ron and Mark's book is a fun and compelling ride down the rabbit hole! They certainly did their homework, and it's refreshing to read a book that delves into the enigmas associated with these beings, listing account after account from credible people... many of whom I personally know. He has beaten the path, getting first-hand accounts to offer an intellectual, unbiased assessment on the probable alien connection with Bigfoot that I myself have witnessed as well. For those who have experienced the 'unusual' when in the woods, this book will encourage you... you are not alone. For those who have not experienced anything unusual, the book could easily take you to the edge of that rabbit hole. The book illuminates the stretching of the veil that will soon be open for us to see into the deeper mysteries hanging out in the ethers of a different frequency.

Ron Morehead
Sierra Sounds

Ronald C. Meyer and Mark Reeder have done it again. Their new book, The Bigfoot Alien Connection Revisited, builds upon and continues the research that was first explored in the popular documentary the Bigfoot Alien Connection Revealed. It is a must-read for anyone interested in alternative views of the Bigfoot Phenomenon. You'll be exposed to a fresh perspective that challenges the conventional paradigm of what Bigfoot really is and how he may be connected to something much larger. Believe me, regardless of how you feel about the subject, this book is anything but dull and will challenge the way you think. It contains compelling arguments and thought-provoking ideas throughout its pages. And since we've yet to discover a Sasquatch body, Both Ron and Mark might be on to something.

Doug Hajicek
MonsterQuest Producer

This book is dedicated to our lead paranormal investigator, Alan Megargle, without whom this book would not have been possible.

Some cutting-edge thinkers suggest that the scientific method has reached its limit in terms of making discoveries and now a new framework or paradigm for knowing is needed to penetrate the truths behind life and intelligence. We hope our book, in a small way, has contributed to this possibility.

CONTENTS

Preface 1

1. Something's Trying to Get Our Attention 7
2. Paranormal Hotspot Locations 11
3. Felt Presence 16
4. Portals 27
5. Sizzled 35
6. Bigfoot and UFOs 49
7. Communications From the Other Side 57
8. Technology and the Paranormal 65
9. Opening a portal 77
   Conclusion 93
   The Bigfoot Alien Connection Revealed 97
   Afterword 99
   Appendices 101
   Appendix A 102
   Appendix B 105
   Appendix C 106
   Appendix D 108
   Appendix E 110
   Appendix: Tools of the Trade 111

Notes 115

PREFACE

In 2016 I was hired by a long-time video distribution company, Mill Creek Entertainment, to produce a series on the phenomenon of Bigfoot. Back then, I knew next to nothing about the large hairy, apelike creature resembling the Himalayan Yeti, supposedly found across America and Canada. Like many people, I had seen the iconic Patterson-Gilman film of a presumed Bigfoot strolling through a section of woods along a creek in Northern California. I was also vaguely aware that the name and figure of Bigfoot were used in marketing a number of products, from coffee mugs to t-shirts. And I had heard of the long-running series on Animal Planet called *Finding Bigfoot*. That was about it.

After doing research on the Internet, the Bigfoot phenomenon appeared to be much more tangible than I had originally believed. So, I accepted Mill Creek's challenge of producing a five-part series titled *Chasing Bigfoot: The Quest for Truth*.

One of the things that surprised me in doing my research was that the fascination with Bigfoot has a long history, going back to the beginning of the 20th century. Called Sasquatch by the indigenous Salish people of the Pacific Northwest, this creature was described as some form of intelligent, forest-dwelling creature. Anthropological literature records account from nearly all Native American cultures of similar spiritual entities. Indeed, Sasquatch myths seem to be deeply seated in the human psyche.

Even more surprising than a belief in Bigfoot across cultures was the discovery of a large modern-day community of Bigfoot contactees and researchers in the United States and many other countries. People were taking the possibility of Bigfoot very seriously, including a small group of respected academic scientists who have devoted parts of their careers to studying every aspect of the mystery behind Bigfoot.

Most of these investigations have centered on cases of physical evidence, such as Bigfoot tracks, which indicate a reality behind Bigfoot sightings. In fact, in many reported cases of Bigfoot sightings, researchers have found footprints at the spot where these sightings occurred.

In the process of producing the series, I did many interviews with people who had direct visual contact with the phenomenon they called Bigfoot. Most were quite detailed and I did not doubt these people had some sort of experience. Usually, the sightings were brief, unexpected and often life-changing. The sightings could have occurred early in life or anytime thereafter. Sometimes multiple people experienced a single sighting. And in nearly every case, people reported a kind of intelligent awareness possessed by the creatures they saw.

One of the more common aspects of these contact experiences was that the Bigfoot appeared out of nowhere and vanished just as suddenly. Not exactly the behavior of animal primates in the wild. This vanishing act on the part of Bigfoot was supported by the fact that Bigfoot tracks were always few in number, seemed to appear out of nowhere, and then suddenly disappeared even when conditions were perfect for footsteps to continue.

There were some other unusual characteristics of contact experiences with Bigfoot. Some people reported an extremely unpleasant smell. One Bigfoot investigator described it as the rank odor of a rotting billy goat. Sometimes ill-defined heat signatures could be seen on infrared sensing devices. Another reported occurrence was eye shine—self-illuminating eyes visible in the dark.

Three other physical signs are interpreted as indicators of the presence of Bigfoot. One is what Bigfoot investigators call *wood knocks* —a distant sound of a tree beaten by a heavy stick. These 'knocks' often occurred in response to a wood knock initiated by a field investigator. In fact, my film crew and I were able to record one of these wood knock responses when out with an investigator in the Rocky Mountains.

The second physical indicators of Bigfoot are vocalizations. The most common are out-of-place howls different than the identifiable cries of wild animals. The most famous of these are Ron Morehead's Sierra sounds. Over a number of years, Ron recorded what sounded eerily like an active exchange in a foreign language between multiple creatures.

Finally, the third physical phenomenon was rocks thrown by an unknown source at investigators or ordinary people hiking or hunting in the woods.

I did not doubt these reports and recordings of unusual animal sounds, wood knocks and rock-throwing were real, but I had no logical explanation for any of them. However, what piqued my interest was an interview I conducted with Jim Myers, owner of the Sasquatch Outpost in Bailey, Colorado. He disclosed that he believed Bigfoot wasn't some flesh and blood, secretive humanoid but something para-physical or interdimensional. That appealed to me since I could not accept the idea of an elusive, undescribed animal behind the Bigfoot phenomenon.

Part of the reason this appealed to me is that I have a long history of paranormal occurrences myself, including a number of non-dual states, out-of-body experiences, direct contact with the great void, some very unusual coincidences and an early obsession with UFOs. I have attended enlightenment intensives, meditation retreats and trained in esoteric martial arts.

On the flip side of the coin, I am the coauthor of peer-reviewed scientific publications in behavioral science and paleontology. I even have a couple of ancient species named after me.

So, the idea of Bigfoot being something supernatural or alien appealed to my scientific and metaphysical curiosity, and I decided to investigate the phenomenon scientifically to look for patterns that might reveal the truth about Bigfoot.

The best way for me to investigate is to produce a documentary feature or write a book on the subject. So, after the release of *Chasing Bigfoot*, it was natural for me to embark upon a documentary feature about the connection between Bigfoot and aliens. I had already written a novel with my longtime writing partner, Mark Reeder, about the possibility of sacred sites having paranormal consequences in the world. So, I enlisted him in writing the sci-fi novel, *Aliens 2035: The End of Technology*, in which we explored the possibility of Bigfoot being one of a number of nonhuman intelligences at play on our planet.

The documentary feature, which I produced with Alan Megargle, was called *The Bigfoot Alien Connection Revealed*, which is also the title of this book. To my surprise, it was highly successful, going viral with over five million views on multiple streaming platforms. In the process of making the movie, I was able to explore many of the ideas floating around on the UFO side of the equation.

It turned out that the huge UFO community has recently morphed into a kind of new religiosity. Fortunately, during our production of *The Bigfoot Alien Connection Revealed*, the government released what are now famous videos of US Navy pilots tracking and engaging some very unusual craft.

The US government later revealed these crafts did not belong to the United States military nor any other country but were, in fact, real. At the same time, I discovered there were several places where Bigfoot, alien crafts and light phenomena occurred together in time and space.

These types of multiple paranormal occurrences became the primary focus of the documentary feature. One of the founding fathers of this idea, Thom Powell, introduced me to the idea of paranormal hotspots. Thom led us on an investigation of one of these hotspots south of Eugene, Oregon, called The Owl Moon Lab.

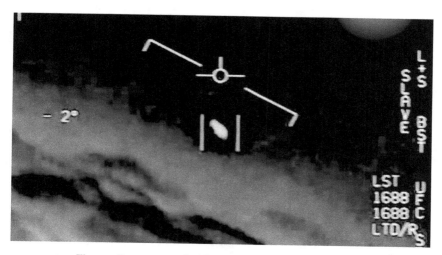

Figure 1: Department of Defense Image of Unidentified Aerial Phenomenon

The Owl Moon Lab had been owned by a retired construction contractor who moved to the area to be near his grandchildren. For the movie, the contractor only wanted to be known as Darrel. After he erected a large metal shed on the property, strange things began to happen. First, Bigfoot knee prints appeared on the backside of his property. Darrel contacted local Bigfoot investigator Tobe Johnson, and almost immediately, multiple paranormal phenomena began to occur. Orbs and typical Unidentified Aerial Phenomena (UAP) and light phenomena happened regularly.

To their surprise, they recorded on a number of occasions sounds that matched well-known Bigfoot vocalizations. Then, unexplained banging noises occurred in the shed during the night. Next, a playful para-physical creature moved objects around and brought synchronistic, meaningful items into their home. Finally, upon the suicide of the son of the former owners, a disembodied voice declared, "I am dead," and some ghostly hand imprints were imprinted on a wall of the house.

To top off our investigation, our lead paranormal investigator Alan Megargle spent some time in the shed, where the unexplained audio activity was occurring. Alan felt a cold wave of energy pass over him while multiple cameras recorded unusual banging sounds with no visible source.

This experience led me to pursue the idea of investigating and filming multiple paranormal hotspots where numerous phenomena reportedly occurred on a regular basis. My film crew and I completed this endeavor in 2022 after two and a half years of investigation.

I again elicited my writing partner, Mark Reeder, and asked him if he would be interested in writing a book about what occurred when investigating nine such paranormal hotspots. Though Mark has experienced several anomalous events in his long life, he remains a paranormal skeptic. Still, the idea of paranormal occurrences, like Bigfoot and ET, as emergent forms of religious phenomena fascinated him, and he agreed.

This book is a record of the many supernormal events we encountered during our filming, as well as the bringing together of the patterns that occurred across these many paranormal hotspots.

1

SOMETHING'S TRYING TO GET OUR ATTENTION

Many people today, particularly in the United States, lead secret lives. What we mean by this is that they have had experiences they can't explain and fit into the life story they tell about themselves. Interestingly, some of these experiences involve alien contact events, UFO sightings and Bigfoot encounters. In many cases, these men and women are what we might call ordinary people but, surprisingly, also some of the greatest thinkers, writers, religious leaders and top-level scientists and technological innovators. They don't usually talk about these experiences for fear of being ridiculed or ostracized by the communities in which they live.

In this book, we use the word 'paranormal' to encompass all the real, but inexplicable occurrences that are in some sense natural but are outside of the normal. One of the themes of the book, perhaps the main theme, is a felt sense that something is trying to get our attention.

Before I began my investigation for the series on Bigfoot, I was in that category of people who had had a number of unexplained occurrences in my life. When I was drawn to the idea that Bigfoot was something para-physical with reported extraordinary supernatural capabilities, it became clear to me that a new approach to understanding the Bigfoot phenomenon was needed.

It was clear to me that if Bigfoot was para-physical, it had to belong in a larger category of para-physical phenomena. For example, author Linda Godfrey has cataloged hundreds of monsters from all corners of the world. This menagerie of beings includes Bigfoot, Dogman, Goatman, Skinwalkers, *Chupacabras*[1], and Thunderbirds. In her book *American Monsters: A History of Monster Lore, Legends, and Sightings in America*, Godfrey argues glimpses of these beings aren't just figments of our overactive imaginations. According to thousands of eyewitnesses, they are temporary manifestations of something real that is completely integrated for a brief period of time into the normal world.

This category of beings that show up unexpectedly can be expanded to include fairies, guardian angels and spirit guides. Observers often report these beings bringing a message or insights from a higher power. Interestingly, Bigfoot contactees often report receiving important life messages.

What about UFOs or UAPs? Strange unidentified craft sightings, sightings of amorphous light phenomena, and telepathic contact with aliens show patterns very similar to glimpses of Bigfoot. These experiences are all unexpected, fairly short and often very meaningful for the individual observer as if he or she had been selected specifically for them.

Then, of course, there is the staple of the paranormal—sightings of ghosts and apparitions of people, most of whom have already died.

These unexplained yet highly documented phenomena led us to ask a very important question: Is it possible these phenomena are in some way connected to the same paranormal source? We wanted to find out in what ways is Bigfoot similar to and different from UFOs or unusual light events or apparitions. Lastly, we were very interested in understanding how the human mind plays a role in all these paranormal occurrences.

What happened at the Owl Moon Lab, described in the introduction, suggested a way my film crew and I could move forward. First, we would identify a number of potential paranormal hotspots. Then, we would investigate and film them. Our hope was that by observing these hotspots through a scientific lens, the paranormal world would reveal itself, and patterns would emerge that shed light on who humans are and what reality is beyond the normal stories we tell ourselves.

To guide our investigations, we used the Skinwalker Ranch[2] as our model. guide. The phenomena recorded at this portal of paranormal activity laid out clear parameters of candidates for our investigations. The first condition was to identify one or more people in each Site who had a history of paranormal experiences and would be willing to act as our guide during the investigation. These folks would have to be willing to appear on camera and talk clearly about the place and its paranormal history. In addition, we asked them to provide us with some evidence in advance of paranormal occurrences. Our goal was to spend at least two days filming at each paranormal hotspot, running some experiments and inviting contact through opening up to what's present beyond our normal senses. Our team always included me, our lead paranormal investigator, Alan Megargle, and occasionally his ghost investigation team, and a camera person.

From a production standpoint, the whole operation was risky. Most times, when film crews follow up on a Bigfoot or UFO sighting or contact with a ghostly apparition, the outcome is disappointing, with no evidence of any significant paranormal phenomena. Mostly, it's like chasing wisps of smoke in the wind. However, to my surprise and relief, multiple paranormal events occurred at each location which we were able to capture on film.

In retrospect, our investigations appeared to be guided by an unseeing hand, or perhaps a guardian angel, who seemed eager to bring these quasi-religious phenomena into the world.

2

PARANORMAL HOTSPOT LOCATIONS

TAKING THE LAB ON THE ROAD

I n the course of our filming, my investigative crew and I made a critical decision. In a radical departure from the usual methods of studying paranormal phenomena, we took our research into the field. We decided to use each paranormal hotspot as its own test site,

Our conjecture was that since Bigfoot, UFOs, Extraterrestrials and other paranormal phenomena don't make appearances in scientific research facilities, we planned to make each site we visited its own window into the paranormal. Our contacts at each of the paranormal hotspots agreed to participate in our filming.

Below is a list of the paranormal hotspots we visited and the individuals associated with each one.

Site L1. The Montana Vortex and House of Mystery are located in Columbia Falls, Montana, just outside of Glacier National Park. Run by Joe and Tammy Hauser, longtime Bigfoot researchers, the Montana Vortex is home to gravitational anomalies and other paranormal phenomena, particularly orbs. During our visit, Joe produced an image captured by one of his cameras in the House of Mystery. He believes it is a glimpse of the Bigfoot he regularly has contact with. At the spot Joe pointed out to us, where he often has a felt presence of the Bigfoot, we filmed a strange, fairy-like creature as filmed in Chapter Six – Bigfoot and UFOS.

Site L2. Bailey is a small mountain town in central Colorado. Over the last ten years, Jim Myers has developed one of the top tourist attractions and Bigfoot research facilities in the region—the Sasquatch Outpost. The Outpost includes a Sasquatch Encounter Discovery Museum as well as a storefront selling Bigfoot merchandise. Some paranormal researchers believe Jim has been channeling the physical manifestation of the Sasquatch Outpost. In creating the facility, he has turned the greater Bailey area into one of the more active paranormal hotspots in the country, including many Bigfoot contact experiences. While conducting our independent research at Jim's store, we were able to make contact with the force or being that is compelling the creation of the Sasquatch Outpost, as well as observing an amazing orb phenomenon.

Site L3. Contiguous with Rocky Mountain National Park, 'The Land' is a forty-acre property where we were able to find evidence pointing to the presence of a paraphysical Bigfoot. In addition, we were able to open what could only be described as a portal and capture on film otherworldly creatures.

Site L4. Cheyenne, Wyoming, is one of the last of the old Western towns and is heralded as the most haunted city in America. Angel and José operate a paranormal investigation enterprise, Paranormal Hunting and Observation Group. PHOG brings a Christian perspective to contact and interaction with apparitions. We joined them for a paranormal investigation in the Historic Plains Hotel, a cultural landmark in downtown Cheyenne.

Cheyenne is also home to FE Warren Air Force Base. Part of the

Global Strike Command, Warren controls one-third of our nation's land-based nuclear missile deterrent. Since the deployment of the nuclear missile silos, this area has become a hotbed of documented cases of UFO and ET activities, as well as cattle mutilations.

Site L5. A large section of land outside Centralia, Washington, is owned by Eira Wulfnothsson, a sensitive and one of the world's leading mystery-school scholars. Here we encountered what could be best described as an alien portal. In addition, Eira also led us on a field trip to nearby Mima Mounds Natural Area Preserve. Of unknown origin, the Mounds are one of the world's greatest unexplained physical anomalies.

Figure 2: Mima Mounds Natural Area Preserve is a state-protected Natural Area in southwest Washington state.

Site L6. Thom Powell, a scientific Bigfoot researcher and an early proponent of paranormal hotspots, lives on a five-acre parcel of land in suburban Portland. Many paranormal events began occurring on his property after he seemed to have brought something paraphysical from the nearby Cascade Mountains onto his land. While there, we witnessed, with the help of two sensitives, a great deal of paranormal activity. One extraordinary event occurred when what one sensitive described as alien inscribed rocks produced high levels of electromagnetic radiation. Inexplicably, the energy was briefly transferable to all present.

Site L7. Board Camp Crystal Mine in the Ouachita Mountains of Arkansas is owned by Cheryl and Orval Murphy. We were drawn to this place by videos of rocks levitating, unusual light phenomena occurring regularly, and the usual telltale signs of a Bigfoot presence. At this site, we were not only able to confirm what we saw in the footage supplied to us by Cheryl and Orval, but we also experienced a paranormal force affecting our electronics.

Site L8. Jay Bachochin, an experienced Bigfoot investigator, has spent years in the Kettle Moraine State Forest of southeastern Wisconsin. His movie, *Finding Jay*, captured a number of paranormal incidents involving a para-physical Bigfoot, including multiple rocks being thrown from no obvious source at the members of his investigation team. Jay took us to one of his more active spots, where we all had contact with a powerful felt presence.

Site L9. The Beast of Bray Road is one of the best-known so-called monsters in the country. Named for the farm road outside of Elkhorn, Wisconsin, where it was first sighted, the creature is also known as the Wisconsin Werewolf. Jay Bachochin put us in touch with Lee Hampel, who owns the adjacent thirty-five-acre parcel of farmland next to Bray Road. Our search for paranormal activities peaked on Hampel's hayfield. Our investigation produced remarkable UAP footage, and we filmed what might be actual footage of the Bray Road Beast.

Figure 3: Lee Hampel on his farm at Site L3 in southeastern Wisconsin

3

FELT PRESENCE

Pretty much everybody has experienced the phenomenon known as 'felt presence'. The event can unfold something like this. You walk into a room and immediately sense something that makes you feel uncomfortable. In this case, the felt presence has expressed itself as foreboding, as if some kind of negative energy is affecting you physiologically, mentally, and emotionally. The opposite may also be true. The felt presence fosters a welcoming or enlivening feeling. Such positive emotions and mind states often occur in designated holy places or shrines.

Sometimes the felt presence articulates itself as a malevolent or dangerous entity. Other times the felt presence is perceived as a holy being or the manifestation of God.

Since the middle of the 20th century, these felt presences have increasingly been interpreted as a para-physical beings such as either Bigfoot or some form of extraterrestrial intelligence. We would argue that every person has the ability to receive this kind of communication.

In our investigations, we uncovered evidence supported by the paranormal literature, supporting the contention that sensing another aspect of reality is a skill some people have naturally and others have developed over time. Throughout history, this skill has been ascribed to sensitives, psychics and mediums.

Many have described this sensing skill as a seventh sense associated with the body as a kind of information processing system, which is why these experiences are always felt. When the contact experience is extraordinary, it is hard to describe to those who have not developed this skill adequately. Interestingly, throughout history, the people who have developed this skill are often the most creative. Individuals like Mozart, Newton, Descartes, Da Vinci, Einstein, Mark Twain, Steve Jobs and many other people in the space and tech sectors.

For example, Eira Wulfnothsson, a worldwide recognized sensitive trained in many of the ancient mystery arts[1], explained to us on a tour of her Centralia Washington property, adjacent to Mima Mounds Natural Area Preserve, that she felt the presence of beings watching us as we walked through a particular wooded area. She seemed quite disappointed after pointing out this phenomenon that none of us had experienced what she had sensed. As an aside, the next day, when we did an interview with Eira, we recorded on video what appeared to be ectoplasm exuding from the side of her body, supporting her claim to mediumship.

At Site L6, Thom Powell's property, Thom led us to a place that essentially encompasses a small piece of the Pacific Northwest's temperate rainforest. He explained that one evening, he strongly sensed something walking down the side of a heavily wooded hill. Thom claimed, "It came crashing down the slope, and so I was waiting and waiting for it to go by, but nothing moved, so I thought maybe I didn't hear it after all. So, I started walking down the trail and then it starts moving again so I jumped on the bench just to get out of its way and then it starts walking softly. Suddenly it was like a blanket was thrown over my eyes and I couldn't see anything. I couldn't even make out trees in the forest. I could almost hear it breathing, it was so close. Then suddenly, something flicked the back of my ear. I jump off the bench and hightailed it back to the house."

Figure 4: Thom Powell (left) talking with Alan Megargle about his Bigfoot experience at Site L3 outside of Portland, Oregon

Punctuating the experience, when he returned to his house, he and his ex-wife heard a loud, unusual scream coming from the area he had just left.

We arranged to bring a local paranormal sensitive, Tish Paquette, to the property. At the spot where Thom had his experience, she immediately detected the presence of beings, which she described as friendly Bigfoot. She felt them to be caretakers of the land Thom owned and okay with our activities. Like Eira Wulfnothsson, she reported a type of higher energy blanketing Thom's property, though none of our crew felt the energy she described.

As evening set in, Alan Megargle and Tish headed to the bench where Thom stood during his experience. Alan recounted what happened next.

"We settled in. I closed my eyes and it wasn't long before we heard a noise at the top of the hill behind us. It let me know that something was there. Tish said that she could sense the presence of something she said was a Bigfoot. She said it was watching us and the rest of the crew at Thom's campsite. She said it knew why we were there. At that time, I could hear these very soft bipedal footsteps. By this time, my eyes are closed and I'm just focusing on the energy of the presence of something. I could feel the energy of the being walk up to within 6 feet of me. There was sort of a warmness in my chest. Then I could feel the energies begin to swirl around as. Then the felt sense of presence just disappeared and when I opened my eyes everything looked white for about five minutes and then things returned to normal."

Interestingly, both Alan and Thom experienced a visual aftereffect of the felt presence. This was just one of three remarkable paranormal events that occurred at Site L6.

At Site L7, the Board Camp Crystal Mine in the Ouachita Mountains of Arkansas, a similar kind of felt presence event occurred. The crystal mine is one of a number of quartz crystal mines in the region. In 2017 the owners, Orval and Cheryl Murphy, had an amazing light phenomena occur over the first crystal deposit they opened up for tourists to enter and collect specimens. At the time of the event, both claimed to have no interest in the paranormal. What they witnessed puzzled them and they had no idea who to contact regarding the strange phenomenon. Eventually, they brought in MUFON—the Mutual UFO Network. MUFON's team of investigators discovered that all the iron posts and other iron-based objects around the site had become deeply magnetized. From that point on, this initial crystal mine was called 'The Event Site'.

Figure 5: Orval and Cheryl Murphy with casts of Bigfoot prints at Site L7, the Board Camp Crystal Mine in the Ouachita Mountains of Arkansas

Soon after observing these strange pillars of light, Cheryl and Orval set up cameras to record any anomalous occurrences on their property. In addition to the anomalous magnetism described by MUFON, their cameras filmed rocks rising into the air and hovering. In fact, so many paranormal phenomena occurred on a regular basis that the two owners began offering paranormal tours in addition to digging crystals.

The Board Camp Crystal Mine appeared to be all about rocks. After viewing recordings of several unexplained rock events that have occurred on the property, we discovered for ourselves the truth of the statement.

The first night of our stay at the mine, Orval and a local Native American who worked there, escorted Alan and our cameraman Paul Lee to the Event Site. Shortly after arriving, Alan felt the presence he had connected with on Thom Powell's property in Oregon. The powerful presence began drawing him down a trail beside the mine. Orval told Alan to "go with it." Alan had his camera running and the other three men followed at a distance.

Figure 6: The initial light phenomenon at Site L7, Board Camp Crystal
Mine, in the Ouachita Mountains of Arkansas

Alan described what happened next. "I was at the event site. Orval said, 'Ask what you want.' I said, 'I came here for contact.' Then there was that sort of gut feeling there was something just beyond where I could see. I walked around the backside of The Event Site. I felt like that was where I needed to go. Down in this ravine off the trail, it sounded like a very substantial rock was dropped four or five feet straight down. It didn't go through the trees. It didn't fall on its own. Something did that."

Shortly after the rock-dropping experience, everybody heard the same unearthly howl which had been recorded at the property days earlier.

The next day the film crew visited the spot where Alan had his experience. Alan and Orval went down into the twenty-five-foot ravine and were able to duplicate the dropping of a particular rock that matched what was heard the night before. We tried to throw a rock into the ravine, but the heavy brush and tree cover made it impossible. In a most unusual way, Alan got the Bigfoot contact he had been looking for.

The rock-dropping experience was not the only paranormal event we experienced at the crystal mine, which will be described in later chapters.

It had been clear for some time that Alan had been striving to develop his seventh sense for paranormal contact. His next opportunity to experience the 'felt presence' came when we traveled to Site L8 in the Kettle Moraine State Forest of southeastern Wisconsin. Here we met up with Jay Bachochin, a long-time Bigfoot researcher who, after a number of years in the field, shifted his theory of Bigfoot from a hairy, ape-like creature to the idea that Bigfoot is a paranormal entity. This switch is a belief more and more Bigfoot researchers are embracing. In his search for the truth about Bigfoot, Jay had a number of unexplained events that caused him to abandon the certainty that Bigfoot was some sort of living, breathing primate.

The last night on our visit to Wisconsin, Jay took us to a place in the Kettle Moraine Forest, which he described as his most active paranormal spot. Alan, our cameraman Paul Lee and myself followed Jay as he led us along a trail, climbing up a ridge between what is known as Kettle Lakes. Clear skies, calm winds and moderate temperatures made the evening comfortable. As we proceeded along the trail, Alan and Jay felt something moving with us to our right.

Alan whispered, "Something came from the other side and crossed over. It's to my right. If I had to guess, directly to my right straight down."

Jay replied, "I felt it on the left side when we were walking in."

Alan added, "Unless every tree dropped something as we walked by, there's something down there."

"It's possible but not plausible," Jay added.

We agreed to settle in a spot along the trail and wait. Alan moved slightly down the hill and sat down. Paul Lee kept his camera rolling on Alan. Jay walked up the trail a bit further and I felt something telling me to perform a letting go meditation to lift the veil that blinds us to the truth.

After a while, we all gathered to talk about what happened to each of us. Jay, who carried a plethora of equipment running at all times, heard what he described as *mindspeak*, telling him to turn off his equipment. "I can tell you right now, I have no equipment running," Jay said. "You haven't seen me do that out here and it felt really good to unplug to get in touch with the nature of what's out here. It's a very calming feeling, I'm as comfortable as I've ever felt in the presence of something inexplicable. It's been an honor coming out here with you guys investigating this way."

Figure 7: Alan Megargle (left) and Jay Bachochin debriefing at Site L8 in the Kettle Moraine State Forest of southeastern Wisconsin

Alan reported, "I felt the surroundings and the thing that was out here, and I felt a connection with it."

Paul, who never felt calm in the woods at night, had a different feeling. "I do feel like I just had a nice long nap. All fear of being out here in the woods just disappeared."

As for myself, being an older person, I felt like I was twenty years old again and bounded back down the trail like I hadn't done in years.

For each of us in our own unique way whatever we had sensed released a knot holding back awareness of what we truly are. Was that one of the many ways paranormal Bigfoot can connect with us?

Whatever it was, it showed an ability to produce a shared experience.

It's important to point out a particular pattern that has emerged in these experiences. In addition to the felt sense of some unexplained nonvisual presence, these experiences are often accompanied by sounds—the sounds of footsteps, of rocks being thrown, of trees being snapped—giving credence to the reality of the experience.

At Site L4 in Cheyenne, Wyoming, we worked with a sensitive whose seventh sense allowed her to feel the presence of people who had passed on.

Our hosts in Cheyenne, Angel Mondello and José Gonzales operate a Christian-oriented, local paranormal investigation enterprise. Besides leading ghost tours in Cheyenne, they practice helping souls, as they said, crossover to the other side.

Figure 8: José Gonzales and Angel Mondello at Site L4, Cheyenne, Wyoming

Angel has had the ability to sense spirits as a young child. "When I was 12 years old, I thought everybody could speak to the spirits that had passed. I thought everybody whose family members that had passed could speak to you. My father who had the ability, too, he explained to me that not everybody can do that and that it is a gift that God gave you."

We were invited to join José and Angel in a paranormal investigation of the most haunted room in the historic Plains Hotel. Room 444, known as Rosie's room, was the room a young bride and her just married husband occupied on their wedding night. Rosie's husband went down for a drink and hooked up with a lady of the evening. When Rosie discovered what was happening, she killed them both and then returned to her room and committed suicide.

We kept the story of Rosie from Angel and brought her up to the room. When she entered, we could see that she was overwhelmed by some sort of 'felt presence'. Angel was shaking as she said, "I'm feeling, like really jittery and really nervous, really scared." Angel then described to us the residual energy of a number of bad things that happened in Room 444 over the years. Finally, after settling down, she was able to feel the presence of Rosie as well as a man named Michael. The team tried to help Michael crossover, but he appeared to be angry and told us through the spirit box to, "Fuck off."

Figure 9: Alan, José and Angel with spirit box in the Plains Hotel at Site L4, Cheyenne, Wyoming

The sensitives we included in our investigations reported that they knew of their unusual ability to sense beyond the brain and body's normal sensory inputs. However, they had no context to interpret and use their seventh sense. Like Angel, they thought for a long-time everybody had this seventh sense ability.

The important question is how many people are there that actually have a highly developed seventh sense and have had to hide it all their lives, perhaps to the point where the ability diminished or was even extinguished.

Bringing this into a broad religious context, all religions have something to say about the nature of humans. Whether it's God's children, manifestations of the all or an individualized, everlasting soul, these religious interpretations give meaning to people's lives and, maybe even more importantly, what happens beyond death. Our experiences at these paranormal hotspot sites indicate that as humans, we are much more than we think we are. This expanded sense of what it means to be human is a major component of the emerging religiosity, often described as spiritual but not religious.

4

PORTALS

A favorite theme of science fiction is an extraordinary opening in space or time that connects us to other beings and realms. Known as portals, vortexes and wormholes, these openings are shortcuts or doorways into the paranormal.

The UFO and Bigfoot communities report numerous accounts of sudden appearances and disappearances by alien crafts and Bigfoot. They are often described as 'appearing out of nowhere' and 'vanishing in the blink of an eye'.

We recorded one typical experience at Site L2, the Sasquatch Outpost in Bailey, Colorado. James Urlacher, a tough, no-nonsense biker, recounted his Bigfoot-portal experience this way. "Everybody in my family saw it was walking into a clearing, it was lit up by the sun, there were trees about 20 yards apart, and it was walking in between them, there was a shimmer that began as a circle, it began shrinking. The Bigfoot kept walking and as the Bigfoot got to the center of the shimmer, it just went away, it just vanished. Everybody got excited. We couldn't believe what we just saw, it was really a life-changing experience for me."

Among paranormal researchers, the sudden appearance-disappearance of a UFO or Bigfoot is often explained by the theory of interdimensional travel. These beings and crafts use portals or wormholes to pop into and out of our world from another dimension. This case was made in the highly successful History Channel television documentary series *Secrets of the Skinwalker Ranch*[1]. The numerous paranormal phenomena documented at the ranch were based on the idea that the land, owned in 2022 by Utah real estate tycoon Brandon Fugal, encompasses a portal or wormhole capable of letting paranormal phenomena pass into our world.

In fact, physicists have used Einstein's Theory of General Relativity to mathematically predict the existence of wormholes. Known as Einstein-Rosen Bridges, these wormholes or portals connect two distant points in space and time via a tunnel.

In addition, recently, scientists have confirmed the existence of magnetic portals. In 2017 NASA scientist Dr. Tony Phillips wrote, "Observations by NASA's THEMIS spacecraft and Europe's Cluster probes suggest that these magnetic portals open and close dozens of times each day. Most portals are small and short-lived; others are yawning, vast, and sustained. Tons of energetic particles can flow through the openings."

Plasma physicist Jack Scudder of the University of Iowa also notes, "Magnetic portals are invisible, unstable, and elusive. They open and close without warning and there are no signposts to guide us to the locations."

It has also been well-documented that certain materials and particles can distort and fluctuate the intensity or direction of the Earth's magnetic field in particular locations on the planet.

Other scientists speculate that what many paranormal investigators and physicists refer to as 'the other side' is much colder. Suppose the portal only allows energy transfer, so matter can't pass through. In that case, would the portal appear as a very dark and cold spot in our world?

While many of us envision portals as spherical openings, they can take on many forms, including tears or rips between worlds or a mesh of multiple holes over an area. Our investigations shed some light on the portal phenomenon.

In the second season of the *Secrets of Skin Walker Ranch*, many of the paranormal phenomena centered around an old, abandoned building that had been home to a 19th-century pioneering family. During one of the numerous outbreaks of paranormal activity at the Pioneer Homestead, the research team, using an infrared thermal detecting device, recorded what was described as an extreme cold spot at the Homestead structure. Could the cold spot signal the opening of a portal, granting strange paranormal phenomena entrance to the ranch? This association of cold spots with portals put us on alert to look for similar cold spot phenomena.

Our team's first encounter with a cold spot indicating a possible portal occurred on a warm, calm July evening at Site L5 during our tour of Eira Wulfnothsson's property, which she said was rife with paranormal phenomena. At one point, she took us to an opening in the woods, where we all experienced a dramatic chill as soon as we entered. Using our thermal sensing device, we were able to pinpoint an area of intense cold, which we recorded on camera. The area's ambient temperature was seventy degrees, however, the cold spot registered between thirty-two and forty-two degrees. We next tested the thermal device on ourselves, and we registered as normal, warm-blooded human beings.

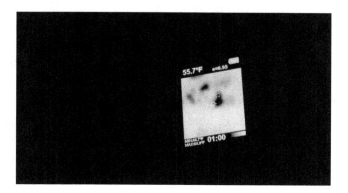

Figure 10: Thermal image of cold spot taken on property owned by Eira Wulfnothsson in Centralia, Washington

Later, studying the footage recorded by the thermal device, we saw what appeared to some of us as the face of a dog. When we sent the thermal image to Eira, who is a renowned sensitive, she observed, "From my earliest memories, I have been connected to the spirit or archetype of the canine. sometimes when others detect the presence of Bigfoot, I sense something canine in nature."

Three months later, we took our investigation in southeastern Wisconsin to the thirty-five-acre farmstead of Lee Hemphill, located near Elkhorn, home of Site L9 and the famous Beast of Bray Road. Here, on another warm, calm night, we identified a place, which we called our 'sweet spot', along the north fence line closest to Bray Road.

At the sweet spot, the vegetation marking the property boundary was an impenetrable bramble of shrubs and trees. Lee recounted a couple of times when he saw a strange animal of some kind walk straight through the brambles as if they weren't physically there. In addition, he also recorded footprints in the snow of something walking through the brambles.

We asked Lee if he would ever go in there and he replied, "No way." When asked why, he answered, "That's where the Beast of Bray Road is." For over seventy years, the Beast of Bray Road has been described on many occasions by area locals as a Dogman of varying sizes.

When we told Lee this is where we were going to focus our investigation, he said, "People don't last long here, so good luck."

For our investigation, we were joined by Jay Bachochin, a dedicated Bigfoot researcher who always travels with the gear necessary to document paranormal encounters.

On that night, while we were setting up our equipment, Jay and the cameraman, Paul Lee, heard something bipedal moving in the brambles. Grabbing the camera and thermal detector, Alan and I took readings. To our surprise, a cold spot hovered above the brambles. Compared to the ambient air temperature of around sixty-five degrees, the cold spot registered forty-two degrees. We recorded for approximately three minutes, with the cold spot slightly changing shape. Was it a portal that had let something come through? Was it the Beast of Bray Road? Further events that night suggested it may have indeed been a portal of some kind.

Figure 11: Alan Megargle holding cast of Bigfoot print made during Bigfoot Adventure Weekend at Site L2 in Bailey, Colorado

A different kind of portal event occurred at Site L2 in Bailey, Colorado. Each year Jim Myers, owner of the Sasquatch Outpost, and Alan Megargle, our lead paranormal investigator, host a three-day event called Bigfoot Adventure Weekend. People from all over the country come to camp out and learn everything they can about Bigfoot. During the long weekend event, experienced Bigfoot researchers lead small groups of participants into the field in hope of contact with Bigfoot.

In 2020 in the course of a daytime scouting expedition to a wooded ridge about ten miles from Bailey, a single Bigfoot print was found and cast.

That night a group led by Bigfoot researcher Kenny Collins returned to the ridge. Joining Kenny was Eric, a Navajo Native American, and Arthur Wach, a rancher from Nebraska.

Arthur described what happened in these words. "I heard something coming up the side of the ridge coming towards us. I could tell it was bipedal, whatever it was. Here comes Kenny beside me with his night vision. He's looking down at it and says, 'Oh my God'."

Kenny picked up the story at this point. "Something drew me to this place and I'm looking at this rock and I see this opening coming. I set down my night vision and take my camera and take a picture. I am mesmerized. I see this opening like this hole. When I come back and look at my picture, there is a large blue orb."

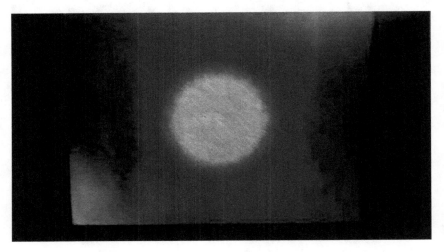

Figure 12: Photo of a blue orb taken by Kenny Collins during Bigfoot Adventure Weekend at Site L2, Bailey, Colorado

At the same time, Arthur also saw something. "I got my phone out and I clicked it and I just took a picture. I didn't think I had anything." Snapping his picture in total darkness with no infrared function on his phone, Arthur captured a most remarkable image—a blue-green circular object containing a complex geometric design within.

For Kenny, the event wasn't over. "So, I run over and get on this rock and use my night vision scope and I'm scoping the spot and here comes a bipedal creature about 5 foot tall and it runs by me. Eric, sitting on a rock nearby beating on a drum, said he saw big one not a little one."

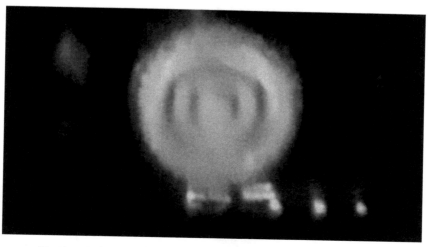

Figure 13: Arthur Wach's picture of a strange geometric shape taken during
Bigfoot Adventure Weekend at Site L2, Bailey, Colorado

Then something unusual happened to Eric. He appeared struck dumb and could no longer remember any of his traditional Native American songs.

Had Kenny and Arthur experienced and photographed for the first time a portal opening up in the form of an orb from two different perspectives? Kenny's photograph was a full-frame amorphous circle. Skeptics could easily say this was either backscatter or some small light phenomena out of focus.

However, for Arthur's picture, neither of these explanations work because of the detailed structure of the object captured in the photograph. In fact, the unusual structure Arthur captured matches many of the UAPs documented in Luis Elizondo's History Channel Series *Unidentified: Inside America's UFO Investigation*. Arthur's photographic feat is even more remarkable considering Elizondo is the former head of the US government's Advanced Aerospace Threat Identification Program.[2]

The main pattern that emerged regarding portals is that they are always connected to other paranormal phenomena. In particular, we noted that portals are often associated with the appearance and disappearance of Bigfoot. In addition, many of these appearance and disappearance events have a connection to what are described as orbs, which some researchers have concluded are visual manifestations of portals. In any case, it would not be unreasonable to conclude that portals have a physical appearance that is measurable. Perhaps, it could even be said that these portals have a technological aspect.

It has been suggested that non-human, non-terrestrial intelligences use portals to send through avatars to interact with us. Indeed, throughout history, anomalous religious events have often begun with the words 'the sky opened up,' indicating the beginning of some mystical experience.

For example, in Revelation 4:1, the Apostle John revealed, "After this, I looked, and behold, a door standing open in heaven! And the first voice, which I had heard speaking to me like a trumpet, said, 'Come up here, and I will show you what must take place after this.' At once, I was in the Spirit, and behold, a throne stood in heaven, with one seated on the throne. And he who sat there had the appearance of jasper and carnelian, and around the throne was a rainbow that had the appearance of an emerald."

The Books of Kings describes the prophet Elijah being taken to heaven in a whirlwind. And the Prophet Mohammed reportedly said that during the Muslim holy month of Ramadan, the gates of heaven are open.

These mystical experiences show a gateway, or portal of some kind, in the sky opens to heaven, which could also be another way to describe other worlds and/or dimensions.

The book's final chapter, 'Opening a Portal', will tell the story of how the team acted not only as investigators of an existing hotspot but actively pursued opening a portal to see if they could film the other side or at least film something coming through from another dimension.

5

SIZZLED

There are many cases of unexplained, temporary physiological and mental episodes associated with paranormal contact experiences. For example, nausea, headaches, vertigo and disorientation are often reported as a kind of unusual effects associated with Bigfoot. Bigfoot researchers have suggested this results from the ability of Bigfoot to produce infrasound—sound waves with a frequency below the normal spectrum of humans' capability to hear. In episodes of Travel Channel's hit series *Expedition Bigfoot* and History Channel's *The Secrets of Skin Walker Ranch*, participants and investigators had to remove themselves from the locations because of the sudden onset of unexplained illnesses.

Another well-documented effect associated with paranormal contact experiences is the loss of cognitive functions, in particular, memory loss. Memory loss is particularly prevalent in UFO abduction cases and other forms of direct contact with extraterrestrials and alien crafts.

Interestingly, these types of effects from contact experiences have been studied extensively since they appear to mimic existing forms of cognitive impairment, including hallucinations, mental illness, schizophrenia and even demonic possession. No doubt, these kinds of effects of an encounter with the paranormal are of concern to science and religion since these are real-world effects demanding to be either explained or dismissed.

In the paranormal as well as the scientific literature, we found no accepted general term to describe these extraordinary physiological and mental disturbances associated with contact experiences. However, we discovered the term 'sizzled' is often used among Bigfoot researchers to describe the temporary loss of cognitive functions. As a result, for this book, we decided the term 'sizzled' aptly captured the inexplicable lapses of memory and strange cognitive impairments we encountered in the five cases we investigated during our filming.

In the chapter on portals, we described the case of a Navajo man named Eric who lost his ability to remember the Native American songs he had been drumming during the appearance of an orb at the Bigfoot adventure weekend outside of Bailey, Colorado. In addition to the orb photographed by Kenny Collins and Arthur Wach, Kenny and Eric described what they thought was a Bigfoot-like creature coming through the orb.

Interestingly, only Eric was affected by the appearance of the creature; neither Arthur nor Kenny reported any 'sizzled' effects. Indeed, in many of these 'sizzling' events, one of the more interesting patterns to emerge is that the cognitive and physical impairments usually affect only one of the people present. It's as if the 'sizzling' was tailor-made for a single individual. In fact, in the case of Travel Channel's *Expedition Bigfoot* series and History Channel's *Skinwalker Ranch* series, the 'sizzling' affected just one of the many team members involved in the investigations.

Another 'sizzled' incident at Site L2 was reported by Scott Barta, an experienced Bigfoot researcher and longtime sufferer of tendinitis. Scott explained what happened after he and a couple of friends left objects at their Bigfoot gifting site. "As I left, this charge went through my body and even when I got to the top of the hill, I told these guys, 'Somebody plugged me into an electric socket.' I don't know what the deal was, but I got a really strange charge." Later he noted that his tendinitis had vanished. As for the others in Scott's party, none of them felt anything unusual.

The event was transformative for Scott in his journey from looking for a hairy, ape-like Bigfoot creature hiding in the woods to freely experiencing para-physical Bigfoot however it wanted to interact with contactees.

The next 'sizzled' experience happened to our lead paranormal investigator, Alan Megargle, when he went to investigate the existence of a potential portal at Site L3 in Colorado. The 'Land', a forty-acre parcel adjacent to Rocky Mountain National Park, is a beautiful piece of property bisected by the Little Thompson River. Over three years, we did numerous Bigfoot investigations on this land.

Figure 14: Possible Bigfoot prints at Site L3, 'The Land', near Rocky Mountain National Park in Colorado

At one point, we found footprints in the snow that seemed to be bipedal but not human. Curiously, the tracks appeared out of nowhere from a large anthill. After tracking them for a short distance, the footprints disappeared at the base of a thin tree. The sudden appearance and unexplained vanishing act suggested to us that there might be a portal on the land.

On one of our trips to the land, Alan decided he would make the arduous trek to a distant outcrop, which we believed might contain a portal. When he finally reached the rock formation, he was able to climb up and look into a highly unusual deep, bowl-shaped hole in the middle of the outcrop. When we met him on his way back from his adventure, he described what happened to him.

"On the way up, I got a very intense pain in the side of my face and my eyes started watering and I could hardly breathe, and I just got really disoriented. At the same time, I got really winded, yet the terrain wasn't steep. It wasn't anything to do with exhaustion, but it was hard to fight through it, but I did, and suddenly the effect just went away."

Upon reflection, Alan felt that maybe he wasn't open enough to what had led him to the rock formation. From that point on, he began a process of committing himself, without fear, inviting contact with whatever was present on our land that day.

Scholars who have studied mystery experiences have concluded the mental state that we are in when encountering the paranormal often determines the kind of experience we will have. Negative emotions, such as fear, often produce negative experiences, both mental and physiological. In a positive frame of mind, the experience will be uplifting or even profoundly revelatory.

The most unusual case of 'sizzling' occurred at Site L9 in southeastern Wisconsin on Lee Hampel's thirty-five-acre hayfield next to Bray Road. With Jay Bachochin joining us, we began our investigation after night set in by following the hayfield's south fence line. We parked our vehicle and briefly scanned the area to the south for any thermal anomalies. Everything seemed quite normal.

Earlier, we had determined that the place to focus our investigation was a heavily wooded area, which we labeled the sweet spot, along the north fence line. After a brief discussion, it was decided that Alan Megargle, with his camera, and Jay, with his array of field equipment, would walk across the field to the sweet spot while our cameraman, Paul Lee, and I would drive the long way around to the other side.

When Paul and I arrived, we parked the car and waited for Alan and Jay to meet us. When they arrived, Jay was noticeably out of breath, but everything else seemed normal. Later we discovered that Jay's experience was far from normal.

Later, when Alan, Paul and I returned to Colorado and began editing the footage we shot at Site L9, I noticed two pieces of footage from Alan's camera that he shot while crossing the field with Jay. The first was an on-the-spot interview. I asked Alan what was going on, and he answered that Jay had asked him to turn on the camera because he had something to say.

Figure 15: Self-illuminating light on the left before the car lights were switched off, at the 'Sweet Spot', Site L9 in southeastern Wisconsin on Lee Hampel's thirty-five-acre hayfield next to Bray Road

Jay spoke in a rambling, confusing monologue. "Now you're out here by yourself just in the dark, now you're not going to spend the night, but there is something that really kind of overtakes that fight or flight. You know, because you think that's what you're here for, you're here to research and investigate, but then you start to whether it's in the mind or whatnot there is something that overtakes you. It is this fear of flight or fight to where you just want to be safe because you really don't know what it is."

Jay and Alan walked a little further and, once again, Jay told Alan to turn on his camera. What we could see on the video was Paul and I arriving in our car along the north fence line and turning off our lights.

What remained was a self-illuminated light which was exactly at the sweet spot. After a few seconds, Jay took out his laser pointer and touched the self-illuminating light. It was as if the sweet spot was saying, "Here I am." It was quite exciting for us.

Figure 16: Jay Bachochin's laser beam above the self-illuminating light at the 'Sweet Spot' at Site L9, Lee Hampel's hayfield in southeastern Wisconsin near Bray Road

But what happened next was even more amazing. I called Jay back in Wisconsin and asked him what he had been thinking when he used his laser pointer to touch the self-illuminating light at the sweet spot. To our surprise, Jay said he had no memory of doing it. Quite astounded, I mentioned to him that he did an impromptu interview while crossing the field. He had no memory of talking to Alan either.

Jay asked, "How was the interview?" I replied, "Quite interesting". He said, "That sounds like me." However, he was quite baffled by his memory loss, especially since he told us he had a photographic memory. In fact, Jay was able to describe in great detail everything that happened before and after the field crossing. To this day, Jay remains totally baffled by what happened that night. This is by far one of the most dramatic cases documented on film of being 'sizzled'. Again, as is often the case in other 'sizzling' events, Jay was the only person affected. The entire venture across the hay field had been uneventful for Alan.

A second event at Lee Hampel's property happened that same evening before Alan and Jay crossed the field and Paul and I drove to the sweet spot.

Lee had taken us on a tour of his property earlier. It was then decided that, as it was getting dark, we should go into town at Lake Geneva and get a bite to eat. All five of us, myself, Jay, Alan Lee and the cameraman Paul, climbed into our rental vehicle and got dinner at Mod Pizza. On our way back to Lee's farmstead, we decided we had to drive Bray Road, the main place of the Beast of Bray Road's many sightings. As we drove down the road, I took out my camera and filmed the two-mile trek.

This trip down the road appeared in our documentary series, *The Paranormal Highway*. When Lee and Jay screened the program, they were highly confused when they saw the footage I had filmed along Bray Road because they had no memory of doing that. It was particularly perplexing because they could hear themselves talking as we drove along.

Lee contacted us in March of 2022 and described his befuddlement when viewing the program. After further conversations, it turned out that neither he nor Jay recalled going out for pizza either, although Jay had taken a selfie of us in the restaurant. In my final conversation with Lee Hampel, he said to me, "I no longer know what reality is."

This turned out to be a case where two people were 'sizzled'. Interestingly, Jay got back his memory between the drive down Bray

Road and beginning our investigations and then lost it again in his trek across the open field with Alan Megargle later that night.

The final case of being 'sizzled' came to us in an unusual way. Looking for contacts for investigating of Site L4, Cheyenne, Wyoming, we came across Jill Pope, the premier author of books on paranormal Cheyenne. In addition to writing about the many hauntings in Cheyenne's Wild West-like downtown buildings, she was well aware of the reported UFO activities associated with the missile fields outside of Cheyenne's FE Warren Air Force Base. She told us about the 2010 incident when a major sector of the nuclear missile fields was taken off-line at the same time a UFO was reported above the field and over Cheyenne. As chronicled in the New York Times, the incident reached the desk of President Barak Obama.

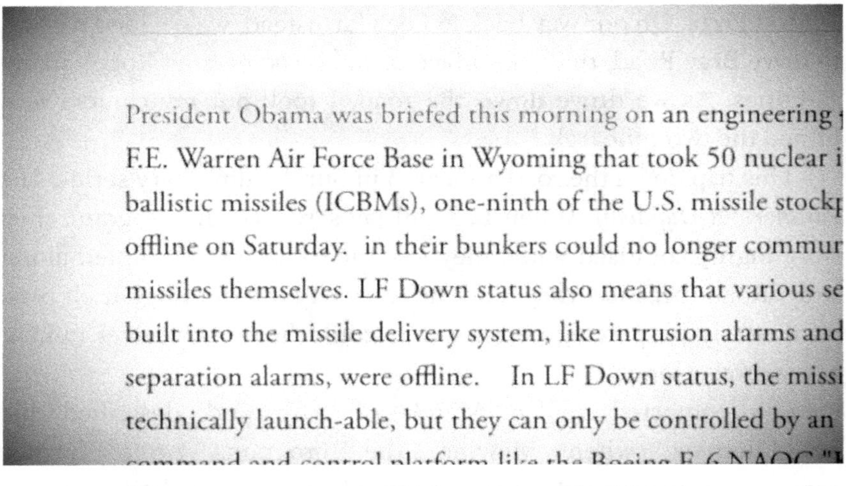

> President Obama was briefed this morning on an engineering [
> F.E. Warren Air Force Base in Wyoming that took 50 nuclear i
> ballistic missiles (ICBMs), one-ninth of the U.S. missile stock[
> offline on Saturday. in their bunkers could no longer commur
> missiles themselves. LF Down status also means that various se
> built into the missile delivery system, like intrusion alarms and
> separation alarms, were offline. In LF Down status, the missi
> technically launch-able, but they can only be controlled by an
> command and control platform like the Boeing E-6 NAOC "I

Figure 17: Excerpt from NYT's article on UFO activity at F.E. Warren Airforce Base outside Cheyenne, Wyoming

Jill also told us about a private surveyor friend who had spotted a UFO over one of the nuclear missile silos. He measured the craft with precision equipment and noticed it did not move for an extended period of time. The final thing he told her was about the arrival of the well-known government black helicopters into the area, at which point he decided it was best to leave.

Jill next mentioned a scientist, Robert Hastings, who wrote the book on the connection between alien crafts appearing above nuclear facilities across the planet. Hastings had interviewed hundreds of ex-military men and women who confirmed this connection between nukes and aliens, particularly in America's nuclear missile fields.

I was able to reach Hastings on the phone and he told me that he was suffering from congestive heart failure and did not feel up to being interviewed. He graciously put me in touch with a former Air Force security policeman who had experienced an amazing UFO-alien encounter that also included being 'sizzled' and was willing to talk about it. Mario Woods' encounter occurred in the now deactivated nuclear missile field west of South Dakota's the Black Hills.

Figure 18: Mario Woods, during his interview

Mario had been stationed at a nuclear missile launch control facility near Sturgis, South Dakota when he stepped outside to smoke a cigarette on an extremely cold November night. "I looked to the East and there was a bright light, not a normal helicopter. I see the object and I thought that's weird. It seemed to be glittering different colors. The size and the intensity of the luminosity was different than anything I've ever seen."

For a short time, Mario used the facility's security lights to flash signals toward the object. It responded in kind while moving slowly to the northeast.

Then around 12:30, the security system's alarm went off in the control facility. Something threatening was happening at one of the missile silos. "It's a Situation Four Alert," Mario explained. "Which is handled differently than just the outer zone penetration of the antennas. It's more serious."

As a result of the alert, Mario and his partner Michael Johnson got their gear and weapons, jumped in their Ford F-150 pickup truck, and headed to the missile silo, designated November 5, about 10 miles away.

Mario explained what he saw as they neared the site. "I could see this glow emanating from the surface and I thought, *what is that?* I've never seen that before. I really don't have an answer for it."

As they rounded the corner to where they could clearly see the missile silo, Mario described an immense object sitting on top of the site. "It honestly looked like a Walmart supercenter on a sphere and it was as bright as any sun I've ever seen a picture of. It had no hard leading edges. Whatever it was, it was covered in a gaseous envelope that just seemed to rotate around it."

Figure 19: Artistic rendering of alien craft above nuclear missile silo as
described by Mario Woods

Michael Johnson, who was driving, positioned the truck just outside the missile site at the beginning of Rancher road that led directly to the nuclear missile silo. "I asked Michael Johnson, 'What is that?' And he was just kind of frozen. I've never seen anybody freeze up like that. He just had his hands locked on the steering wheel."

The two security policemen were supposed to get out of their vehicle and fully investigate what was going on since this was an inner penetration security alert. But they did not get out of the vehicle. Then strange things began to happen.

Mario recalled, "It seemed like time slowed down and the atmosphere in the truck was evacuated. The only way I knew to get relief from whatever it was doing was to roll down the passenger side window. I flashed this thing, whatever it was, with my flashlight. I was asking for relief, I wanted to breathe. And I got relief and I slumped into my seat."

At this point, Mario experienced a form of tunnel vision and his consciousness was not normal. Then he got a strange kind of communication. "I heard these voices but not verbally... like speaking through water, which bothers me still today. I see these beings that are maybe ten feet from my truck. There are two smaller beings and a taller one in the back. I was afraid of that one."

Then Mario blacked out and the next thing he explained, "I saw the side of my security police vehicle. Somehow or another, I'm on my back about 3-4 feet off the ground and then I blacked out again."

Mario's experiences were jumbles of alertness and blankness. He remembered being in some sort of gel and had strong feelings of dread that have haunted him ever since.

Eventually, as Mario tells it, "I open my eyes and am sitting in the truck. Michael Johnson is still sitting there holding the steering wheel. I don't know how much time has passed and I don't know what just transpired and I looked to my right and there's a big white wall about four feet away from us."

The white wall turned out to be the backside of the Newell reservoir dam over ten miles away from the missile silo. Security search teams finally found the two men and escorted them back to the base, debriefed them and for security purposes, closed the book on what happened until recently.

Interestingly, Michael Johnson had no memory of the event and Mario lost track of him. This appears to us to be a clear case of being 'sizzled' and if what Mario described actually happened, he definitely experienced a form of alien contact. In addition, once again, it represents how two people in the presence of an anomalous appearance have very different experiences.

As part of what's being called the religion of no religion or a spiritual but not religious movement, our investigation supports the idea that being 'sizzled' is not about believing or not believing but noticing how being 'sizzled' powerfully affects the lives of individuals who have had the experience and the communities to which they belong. Throughout history, many individuals have been struck dumb or wise by the presence of the divine or the invisible in the world.

Saint Francis of Assisi had a profound moment of inspiration from the divine. One day while riding through fields beyond the walls of the town, he saw a disfigured man coming toward him. The man's unbearable stench told Francis he was a leper, the foulest of the foul, who must be avoided because leprosy was a very contagious disease. But instead of leaving, Francis dismounted from his horse and kissed the leper with the kiss of love. Once more on horseback, he turned to greet the leper, but the man had vanished. Francis determined the leper was Jesus Christ, who descended to earth to receive a kiss from his servant. In his will, Francis wrote, "When I was in sin, too bitter to me seemed to see the lepers, and the Lord led me among them, when I left, what first estimation bitter, I was changed into sweetness of soul and body, and after I left the world."

The Bible's Acts 9 relates the conversion of Saul of Tarsus to the Apostle Paul, showing how encounters affect people differently.

Saul was still breathing out murderous threats against the Lord's disciples. He went to the high priest and asked him for letters to the synagogues in Damascus so that if he found any there who belonged to the Way, whether men or women, he might take them as prisoners to Jerusalem. As he neared Damascus on his journey, suddenly, a light from heaven flashed around him. He fell to the ground and heard a voice say to him, "Saul, Saul, why do you persecute me?"

"Who are you, Lord?" Saul asked.

"I am Jesus, whom you are persecuting," he replied. "Now get up and go into the city, and you will be told what you must do."

The men traveling with Saul stood there speechless; they heard the sound but did not see anyone.

Saul got up from the ground, but when he opened his eyes, he could see nothing. So, they led him by the hand into Damascus. For three days, he was blind, and did not eat or drink anything.

In Damascus, there was a disciple named Ananias. The Lord called to him in a vision, "Ananias!" "Yes, Lord," he answered.

The Lord told him, "Go to the house of Judas on Straight Street and ask for a man from Tarsus named Saul, for he is praying. In a vision, he has seen a man named Ananias come and place his hands on him to restore his sight."

"Lord," Ananias answered, "I have heard many reports about this man and all the harm he has done to your saints in Jerusalem. And he has come here with authority from the chief priests to arrest all who call on your name."

But the Lord said to Ananias, "Go! This man is my chosen instrument to carry my name before the Gentiles and their kings and before the people of Israel. I will show him how much he must suffer for my name."

Then Ananias went to the house and entered it. Placing his hands on Saul, he said, "Brother Saul, the Lord—Jesus, who appeared to you on the road as you were coming here—has sent me so that you may see again and be filled with the Holy Spirit."

Immediately, something like scales fell from Saul's eyes, and he could see again. He got up and was baptized, and after taking some food, he regained his strength. Saul spent several days with the disciples in Damascus. At once, he began to preach in the synagogues that Jesus is the Son of God.

It is important to note that experiences such as spying Bigfoot in the wilds or alien abductions can also be described as glimpses into the beyond or journeys to the other side. Among the Native American plains tribes, these journeys are undertaken during a traditional Sun Dance as a means for young men of the tribe to commit themselves to a renewed sense of being and a sense of purpose in helping the community to a better life.

So, it could be said of these 'sizzling' experiences that they are attempts of another dimension to give meaning and information to the lives of those who are briefly connected to a world beyond themselves. In the new religiosity of the paranormal, this is a spiritual endeavor meant to wake people up from a deep numbness to the world around them.

6

BIGFOOT AND UFOS

Perhaps one of the most baffling aspects in connection with cryptids, particularly Bigfoot and UFOs, is the absence of good visual evidence recorded on film, phone cameras or still photos. In spite of thousands of contact experiences with Bigfoot, for example, nothing better than the controversial 1967 Patterson–Gimlin film[1] has surfaced to date. Most amateur videos of UFOs are grainy or, in a number of cases, patently fakes.

On the other hand, the US government has released remarkable videos of alien crafts. Subsequently, interviews with Navy pilots who interacted with these crafts—now called Unidentified Aerial Phenomena or UAPs—have verified these videos as genuine. In interviews, these pilots repeated two recurring themes about these unidentified alien craft. First, they were faster than any technology the earth is currently capable of. Second, the crafts exhibited aware and intelligent behavior.

In an interview my team conducted with paranormal author Rosemary Ellen Guiley[2] for our documentary feature film *The Bigfoot Alien Connection Revealed*, she put an interesting interpretation on these recent contact experiences. "How do these experiences compare with a historical perspective transformation [of] the people through some kind of contact? Looking at the historical contact literature, we have people talking about fairies, about angels, about spiritual masters, religious figures ... coming into contact with them and having suddenly an explosion of change in their consciousness and even in their body and now it's happening in the UFO and Bigfoot arena. So maybe just the clothing of the experience has changed to suit our modern age, but the result is the same an awakening of what spiritual in terms would be called superpowers."

To our amazement, in our investigations, we may have captured on film not only fairies but also Cryptids.

One celebrated cryptid is the Beast of Bray Road, also known as Dogman, located at Site L9 in southeastern Wisconsin. The night of our investigation of this legendary cryptid, we visited Lee Hemphill's thirty-five-acre hayfield next to famed Bray Road. The team focused on a particular location along Lee's North fence line. We called this location the Sweet Spot. Separating this field from Bray Road was an impenetrable bramble of shrubs and small trees.

During the early part of our investigation, described in the 'Portals' and 'Sizzled' chapters, we had good evidence that something paranormal was definitely happening at the sweet spot.

Having placed a REM pod at the edge of the thicket, we took a break and decided to walk north of the Sweet Spot. Strange things continued to happen to our gear, which we describe in the technology chapter.

Believing that we had done all we could do that evening, we returned to the Sweet Spot to retrieve the REM pod. As Alan bent down to pick up the device, he excitedly declared, "Can you not see that, come right in front of me, is something to the right something to the right, something is right over there something is moving, right there, see it... I can get it on camera ..."

What we all could see were two eyes staring back at us.

In spite of all our movements, talking and shining infrared and white lights, some creature stood its ground on all fours just inside the brambles for nearly three minutes. Had we just captured on film the infamous Beast of Bray Road? If not, what was it?

The next day we briefed Lee Hemphill on what happened and this is what he said, "It's not a coyote, raccoons no, you know no animal would come and stay there when you guys are out there, no animal is going to do that."

We asked Lee about the possibility of Dogman not being as large as a full-grown human male. Lee's answer was informative. "There's five different cryptids out here and the one, Dogman, is relatively small. Standing up, he is about 40 inches, if he would be down on all fours, he could easily be low to the ground. I've seen him out in the hayfield and photographed small tracks in the snow walk right through this thicket."

Figure 20: Image of possible Dogman creature captured on film at the 'Sweet Spot' on Lee Hampel's farm, next to Bray Road at Site L9 in southeastern Wisconsin

Once home in our studio, we were able to analyze the footage captured by two cameras of the creature. The eye configuration of the creature was clearly that of a predator. Most remarkably, it had unusually large ears and an elongated body. Both are characteristics often associated with descriptions of the Beast of Bray Road, including what we saw in a remarkable photograph in Lee's possession.

The Beast of Bray Road is most often described by people who have seen it as a seven-foot-tall humanoid covered with fur and with a head resembling a wolf or a bear. It's interesting to think about what might have happened if we had encountered a seven-foot-tall Dogman with a wolf's head. Instead, we witnessed something much smaller, still able to evoke amazement but not fear. It was as if the creature had decided to give us just what we were able to handle while still providing plausible evidence of its existence. If the unknown creature in the thicket did indeed act in this manner, then our encounter was a remarkable demonstration of alien intelligence and para-physical capabilities.

Figure 21: Shadowy figure on right peering at the 'Sweet Spot' taken by Lee Hampel's Trail Cam at Site L9, Lee's farm on Bray Road in southeastern Wisconsin

Figure 22: Pencil-shaped UFOs above the 'Sweet Spot' taken by Lee Hampel's Trail Cam at Site L9, Lee Hampel's farm in southeastern Wisconsin

One of the main reasons we chose Lee Hemphill's hayfield to investigate was a series of trail cam images he had sent to us. The sequence of still frames shows a shadowy half figure with the sort of pointy head often associated with descriptions of Bigfoot. But what was most remarkable was that the camera was pointed directly at our Sweet Spot in the distance. Directly above the Sweet Spot and off to the right are incredible images of pencil-shaped UFOs often associated in ufology literature as motherships. In each frame, the UFOs have changed positions and numbers.

Over the years, hundreds of reports have documented instances of UFOs and Bigfoot occurring together. So, maybe what we have recorded at Site L9 on Bray Road in Wisconsin is a conjunction of alien crafts and Dogman.

As with Lee's Dogman photo, many researchers have pictures and videos of paranormal phenomena they are not yet ready to release to the public. Many see these experiences as personal and not for public consumption. Others fear a backlash from a public not yet ready to accept a paranormal explanation for what have become in the past 100 years everyday occurrences in the United States. Still, others are looking for a big payday.

Such was the case with Joe Hauser at Site L1, the Montana Vortex and House of Mystery. Joe showed us a piece of video footage captured one night on his security cam in the House of Mystery. The camera, filming with infrared, showed a shadowy figure moving inside the House of Mystery that very much resembled the form captured on Lee Hemphill's security camera sequence.

While visiting Joe Hauser, he told us about how he and his wife Tammy have had numerous interactions with what he called his resident Bigfoot. He took us inside the House of Mystery, where the potential Bigfoot filming occurred and began talking about his Bigfoot. "He's big, probably about seven and a half feet tall, big shoulders, narrow waist. He would be a sub-adult now. And he's in here, we're pretty sure, during the summer, sometimes I'll bring a chair up and meet him here, and you can hear like an 800-pound person walking across in here, but there is nobody in here... Or I will come and will hear him walk out like he's already here."

While Joe was explaining his Bigfoot encounter, I stepped outside the Mystery House and began filming through a window, putting the camera on a monopod so that I could record what was happening inside. However, when the team returned to our studio and checked out the footage, we observed the strangest thing. Just as Joe was explaining how big his Bigfoot was, from the lower-left edge of the frame, what can only be described as a pure white, fairy-like moth creature about the size of a fist flew right by everybody and disappeared into the upper right-hand corner of the frame.

This was a cold November day, long past the time when moths would be active. In fact, nearby Glacier National Park lists no moths or butterflies the size of what we captured on video. Interestingly, none of the three people inside the House of Mystery saw anything. The fairy-like creature appeared to be self-illuminated in that it would have been backlit since the sunlight was coming from the other direction.

Many para-physical researchers have noted that whatever Bigfoot is, it seems to have a sense of humor, which is a mark of intelligence. Is it not rather amusing that as Joe was talking about an 800-pound creature, a diminutive fairy moth shows up at that instant?

Figure 23: Fairy/moth entity (lower center of frame) filmed at Site L1, the Montana Vortex and House of Mystery

Once again, paranormal expert Rosemary Ellen Guiley has an interesting take on these types of interactions. "The characteristics that are associated with the para-physical nature of Bigfoot include telepathic communication. People who have had contact experiences with Bigfoot feel that they are intelligent, maybe even superior to human beings. So, you have telepathy, and we have what would be called as bi-location or rapid transport and the natural ability to be here and then suddenly there without visual evidence of getting there, without walking or running. We have footprints that seem to drop from outer space... If the Bigfoot wants to be material, it seems to have the ability to do that and then turn itself into something intangible, as if it is going through an interdimensional doorway. You may call this Bigfoot's ability to shapeshift as reported by many native cultures."

In addition to these encounters with cryptids, we will describe in the chapter 'Opening a Portal' how we captured on a trail cam video unworldly creatures that could only have arrived inter-dimensionally.

7

COMMUNICATIONS FROM THE OTHER SIDE

The history of modern science is replete with cases of great scientific breakthroughs that seem to appear out of thin air as if magically derived. Three of the most famous cases in history are the groundbreaking discoveries made by the 17th-century mathematicians Sir Isaac Newton and Gottfried Wilhelm Leibnitz and the 20th-century physicist Erwin Schrödinger. Newton and Leibnitz simultaneously and independently, through metaphysical means, discovered and developed the theory of calculus. Schrödinger took the emerging quantum physics studies of Bohr, Planck and Einstein and created a partial differential equation that governs the wave function of all quantum mechanical systems. In other words, using the Schrödinger Wave Equation, his wave would become the basis for present-day modern quantum mechanics.

What all three of these groundbreaking and transformative scientists have in common is that their fundamental breakthroughs in mathematics and physics were not simply the result of hard work and observation. Each scientist spoke of receiving their transformational insights as a kind of mystical download of information, which they attributed to an inexplicable power.

In fact, this paranormal process of informational downloading from some source outside the normal paths of human reasoning and creativity has occurred more frequently since the beginning of the modern digital age. Philosophers and parapsychological researchers often refer to this source, which is hidden by some sort of veil, as 'the other side'.

Reports of a secret society of individuals, called the Invisibles, who regularly get downloads and turn them into new digital and biotechnologies, have emerged in the past fifty years. Supposedly unconnected to one another, they nonetheless are responsible for many major breakthroughs of the past seventy years.

Comparative religious studies point to these mystical downloads as the basis of the major religions of the world. Stories told of Moses, Jesus, Buddha and Mohammed emphasize their mystical awakenings occurred during solitary pilgrimages in the wilderness. Case in point, I was told by my enlightenment teacher how he was part of the downloading process that led to the formation of Scientology by a group of men during an opening up ritual in the Mojave Desert.

There are multiple ways to have these downloads. It can happen spontaneously, or as part of a ritual practice, or shutting down certain areas of brain function as a result of psychedelics, exhaustion and meditation.

Another term for these downloads or otherworldly communications is channeling. The practice of channeling—a person's mind being taken over by a paranormal source for the purpose of communication—has been around since humans discovered fire[1].

In the last sixty years, some of the best-known channeling events are Helen Schucman's 1976 best-selling book *A Course in Miracles*, a curriculum for achieving spiritual transformation, and *The Seth Material*, a collection of writing dictated by Jane Roberts to her husband from late 1963 until her death in 1984. According to Roberts, the words were spoken by a discarnate entity named Seth. *The Seth Material* is regarded as one of the cornerstones of New Age philosophy.

In 1952 George Van Tassel claimed to have received messages via telepathic communication from an extraterrestrial and interdimensional being named 'Ashtar'. This ET source became the first documented channeling of an alien being during the age of UFOs.

In the case of Van Tassel's channeling experience, the alien being, Ashtar, provided Tassel with instructions to build the Integratron, a unique structure in Landers, California, near Joshua Tree National Park. According to Tassel and his followers, inside the dome-shaped building, people can experience rejuvenation, anti-gravity and astral travel.

Figure 24: George Van Tassel's Integraton in Landers, California

More recently, Jim Myers, the proprietor of Colorado's Sasquatch Outpost, the focal point of Site L2, channeled the creation of the Outpost. In 2012 after a life of world travel, Jim and his wife took up residence in Bailey, Colorado. In this picturesque mountain town, they purchased the old Mercantile Building and began renovating it so it could function as a local grocery store. Shortly after, Jim's childhood interest in strange creatures was rekindled by two women who reported nearby Bigfoot encounters. As Jim's own Bigfoot experiences grew, he and his wife slowly began turning the Mercantile Store into a Bigfoot merchandising enterprise, which eventually became the Bigfoot Museum and Research Center.

What guided Jim in constantly expanding the outpost is still very mysterious to him. He told us, "I'm open to the idea that my presence here is because I was led to build the outpost in Bailey. Now I'm hoping I'll learn more about that and as time goes on, that understanding will become more apparent to me. I don't think all this happened by chance. We were led in some respect to do all this."

Figure 25: Jim Myers, owner of the Sasquatch Outpost, Site L2 in Bailey, Colorado

Figure 26: Site L2, The Sasquatch Outpost in Bailey, Colorado

During our investigation in Site L2, we decided to see if we could make direct contact with the force or spirit that guided Jim in the creation of the outpost. We brought in a shaman who regularly practiced channeling to see if she could connect with the creative spirit guide. This attempt failed.

Next, we used a spirit box in a session with Jim. Spirit boxes are used to convey the voices of ghosts in places that are believed to be haunted. In ghost hunting parlance, these voices are called EVPs or Electronic Voice Phenomena. With the spirit box running, Jim asked questions such as "Are you the spirit of Bigfoot?" Finally, after many attempts, when Jim started to ask the question "Are you here?", before he could actually finish the question, having only said "are you...", a voice came through the box and completed his sentence with "here".

A couple of other incidents occurred with the spirit box that day when we went to the location described in the chapter on portals where the three men had contact with and photographed an orb. We wanted to see if whatever was guiding Jim in the creation of the Sasquatch Outpost was the same entity as it appeared on the ridge to Arthur, Eric and Kenny. At one point, it seemed as if whatever was present was playing with us and spoke through the spirit box in the

RONALD C. MEYER & MARK REEDER

voice of a child. Finally, when Jim, using dowsing rods, asked whatever was there to point out its location, it seemed to indicate it was everywhere. In frustration, Jim asked, "What should we do now?" A clear and loud voice from the spirit box replied, "Leave." So, we did.

Also, in Bailey is the Glenn Isle Resort and home to the Bigfoot Adventure Weekend. Mary Ruth, the proprietor of Glenn Isle, told us that many visitors reported a female ghost presence in their rooms. Mary Ruth also described, as told in the chapter on technology, an incident where she had her own interaction with this female presence.

On a separate occasion, our paranormal team did a ghost investigation of the resort and once again, there was a clear verbal response and a loud laugh from a female voice. Everyone present was in agreement that this ghostly presence was friendly and wanted to be known as such.

One other case occurred when we used the spirit box at Site L4, Cheyenne's historic Plains Hotel. Working with Angel Mondello and José Gonzales to learn their Christian paranormal investigation techniques, the team ended up in the infamous room 444, known as Rosie's room. Here, the just married Rosie and her husband were spending their honeymoon. When her husband went downstairs for a drink and ended up with a prostitute, Rosie killed them both, then returned to room 444 and committed suicide. When Angel asked Rosie her husband's name, a clear, loud female voice replied, "Rob."[2]

So, if the Sasquatch Outpost is truly being channeled by Jim Myers, it has resulted in a profound example of the other side producing a tangible manifestation in the physical world. As Jim continues to grow the Outpost, Bailey continues to facilitate contact experiences transforming it into a paranormal hotspot, influencing more people every year.

However, the most impactful results of channeling have occurred in the religious domain in the form of sacred texts. According to Exodus 20, Moses led the Israelites, fleeing from Egypt's harsh rule, across the desert toward the Promised Land. During the journey, Moses climbed Mount Sinai, where inspired by God speaking from a burning bush, he wrote down the Ten Commandments on tablets of stone.

In 610 AD, the Prophet Mohammed said he received the first of a series of revelations that would become the Koran, the doctrinal and legislative basis of Islam.

Finally, according to the Church of Jesus Christ of Latter-Day Saints, in 1823, an Angel named Moroni visited Joseph Smith and revealed to him *The Book of Mormon* as written down on golden plates.

Perhaps everyday life is filled with moments of anomalous sounds or visions we have a hard time explaining. It's like when you are in a crowded room such as an airport, conversing with friends and off in the distance, you hear your name called. It's like waking up from a dream.

It's the same with anomalous events. They wake you up from your ordinary dream world. Evolutionarily speaking, we have evolved to pay attention to these anomalies because not paying attention to them could have dramatic, both positive and negative, consequences for the survival of hunter-gatherers. However, cultural and environmental circumstances have changed. As societies have grown and evolved over the intervening millennia, because of the dictates of scientific and religious dogma, these anomalous events are easier to dismiss as something unimportant.

However, these events still have great significance for us, though because of our backgrounds, we may interpret them differently. Such is the famous story of paranormal researcher and lecturer Rey Hernandez and his wife, who together observed an anomalous light phenomenon. Rey interpreted the light as a spaceship and his wife, who is a Christian, saw it as an angel. This led Rey, a former paranormal skeptic, to launch a massive investigation into the source of all paranormal phenomena and create an archive of their occurrences.

So, the occasional guardian angel still appears to some of us, protecting us from danger, a holdover from our Christian past. But these communications from the other side point to an aspect of humanity that demonstrates we are constantly becoming more than religion and science tell us we are.

A while back, I produced a series on the American hunter. Some of the hunters we interviewed during the production told me what they loved about hunting. They loved being in the wilderness, especially when hunting big game. Often hunters told me the same stories: "My ego, the self, slips away. I become one with my body, with the environment and particularly with my prey. I sense everything that's going on in a new way, I sometimes get sacred communications. I am led on the hunt by some invisible force."

Often, I was told that if the hunt was successful, they offered a kind of ritualistic thanks to the animal they killed for the journey the animal took them on and for the sacrifice it made to sustain the hunter's life. This is probably as close as we modern people can get to the experience of our ancient ancestors.

8

TECHNOLOGY AND THE PARANORMAL

 'If we are contacted by an alien intelligence, it will be through their technologies.'

— JACQUES VALLÉE

Cutting-edge thinkers from the domain of theoretical physics, origin of life investigators and artificial intelligence designers have gone on record suggesting that humans, technology and the paranormal are linked and have been co-evolving together since our earliest ancestors appeared in Africa. If true, contact events that often have been interpreted in religious or mystical terms have, in fact, shaped the destiny of humanity and the explosion of technology since the first appearance of consciousness millions of years ago with our earliest hominid ancestors.[1]

In addition, among astrobiologists and astrophysicists, the consensus is that if Earth is being visited or has been visited by alien civilizations, it will not be in the form of biological entities but by their technology. Perhaps, even by technologies unimaginable to us.

In our investigations of multiple paranormal hotspots, the most frequent, the most demonstrable, but hard to explain, anomalous

RONALD C. MEYER & MARK REEDER

occurrences centered on some kind of manipulation of technology. These strange technological events cannot be explained by some kind of mental psychosis or faulty brain chemistry. Instead, these occurrences appear more as a calling card telling us to 'pay attention'. Interestingly, each site we visited exhibited its own unique technological anomaly as we will describe.

Site L1, the Montana Vortex and House of Mystery, did not at first present any technological oddity. Technological interactions were minimal. Then, at one point during our night investigation, Alan's high-powered flashlight went dead in an instant. The fully charged batteries were completely drained.

As it turns out, we discovered that a sudden inexplicable discharge of batteries is one of the most common anomalous events that occur during paranormal investigations. There are no obvious explanations for how this is possible.

In Bailey, Colorado, at Site L2, we set up a spirit box session with Jim Myers, owner of the Sasquatch Outpost, to see if he could contact the force that was guiding him in the creation of the Outpost. A spirit box scans at a constant, fast rate through all the available radio signals on the AM or FM dial. The scanning produces a very clear audible white noise as the spirit box runs through the frequencies. Shortly after turning on the spirit box, something very unexpected happened. A dramatic slowdown of the scan rate occurred for about two seconds.

Our lead paranormal investigator, Alan, who has over 10 years of experience with the technology incorporated in a spirit box, noted at the time, "All right, so just a second here. I've never had that happen before, I'm watching and looking at it. The spirit box scrolls through the different frequencies, you can see the frequencies that it is currently on. For some reason, it just really slowed down as it went through that batch of frequencies. That's never happened before."

Surprisingly, when we returned to our studios in Louisville, Colorado, we saw that the spirit box had also slowed down a couple of seconds just before the incident Alan noticed. This first slowdown occurred the moment when Jim Myers asked his first question. Had the spirit box malfunctioned? None of the other electronics in the outpost showed any change, such as the dimming of lights, and over the next couple of hours of our investigation, the spirit box performed flawlessly.

Did something demonstrate in a tangible way a power over our technology? Was it the force that has been guiding Jim in the creation of the outpost? Is it some sort of alien technology interacting with our technology? Documented incidents such as this one pose questions without answers.

A short distance from the Sasquatch Outpost at Site L2 is the historic Glenn Isle Resort. The proprietor, Mary Ruth, described to us in an interview her own encounter with technological anomalies at the resort. One night while working in one of the cabins, she noticed on her way to the bathroom that the light to the basement was off. She explained, "I said out loud leaving the bathroom, 'If there is a ghost in here, it would be really nice if the light was turned on for me.' When I went to go downstairs, I walked around the corner and the light was on." Later with her hands full of laundry, she wished that the dryer door would open and it opened on its own.

Mary Ruth believes that the ghostly presence is friendly and even helpful, and most importantly, is pleased with their restoration efforts of the old resort.

There is no doubt that the most powerful and perhaps terrifying technological disruption by some mysterious power occurred in 2010 at Site L4 in Cheyenne, Wyoming. It happened in conjunction with observations of alien craft over Cheyenne and the United States' nuclear missile fields controlled by nearby FE Warren Air Force Base.

. . .

Paranormal author, Jill Pope, was in Cheyenne at the time and recalled, "In 2010, there was an outage, or the Air Force said it was like a computer glitch, where they didn't have control of the nuclear missiles. They have 50 missiles at one of their five sites, and they did not have control of those. They reported that it lasted fifty-nine minutes, but many of the airmen spoke out and said it was several hours on and off and this happened in concurrence with UFO sightings above the missile silos. So, many people question if UFOs were the cause of the loss of control."

The loss of nuclear missile control is not some small-scale disruption, like a light being turned on or flashlight batteries draining in an instant. Indeed, it could have been catastrophic and, as such, was well-documented, with the incident reaching the desk of then President Obama.

On a less-grander scale, during our paranormal investigation with Angel Mondello and José Gonzales of room 444 in Cheyenne's Plains Hotel, something unusual occurred as we wrapped up for the evening. Throughout our investigation, both Angel and José felt what they determined was a 'dark' presence in the bathroom and refused to go into the room. At one point, Alan put the REM pod in the bathroom. Nothing happened until the very end of our investigation. The top of the REM pod holds four colorful LED lights that are triggered if there's a sudden temperature shift.

For some reason, José noticed one of the REM pod lights blinked on and he began interacting with the device, saying things like, "I like the blue light. Would you turn it on for me?" The blue came on. When he asked, "You like the green light?" the REM pod switched to the green light. This interaction continued for over two minutes. Was José somehow controlling the REM pod, or was the device controlling him in some kind of mind-technological telepathy? All José would say is that he felt compelled to interact.

Figure 27: Rem pod used in our investigations that interacted with José at Plains Hotel, Site L4, Cheyenne, Wyoming

The most bizarre and inexplicable technological incident during our investigations occurred at Site L6 on the property of Thom Powell, one of the earliest proponents of the idea of paranormal hotspots. During our investigation of his property outside of Portland, Oregon, Thom invited two sensitives, Mitch Townsend and Tish Paquette, to join us.

Mitch, a long-time Bigfoot investigator, brought with him what he described as 'encrypted rocks' he had found in Washington State's Cascade Mountain Range. Mitch allowed us and Tish to examine them. As we handled the seemingly inert stones, Mitch described how he stumbled across them. "I got what I would call a subliminal messaging and it led me to a site on a major regional river in Southwest Washington, and I discovered what we call pictographic stones."

Mitch told us scientists who analyzed the images reported that they were not painted on the stones but inexplicably integrated into the stones' matrix. Mitch hypothesized about the images, "They are actually data chips that were impregnated on the stones at the molecular level. I think what we have is an alien portable library."

After a short time, Alan decided to bring out his tri-field meter to see if we could detect any electromagnetic energy or magnetic readings.

To everyone's astonishment, including Mitch, the rocks broadcast some of the highest radio frequency readings ever detected on Alan's meter. Not only were the rocks emanating radio signals, but if we held one of the rocks for a while, then set it down, each of us, in turn, generated radio frequency pulses. Tish, perhaps because of her sensitive nature, generated the strongest pulses, though we all experienced a physiological shift in our bodies, almost as if we were somehow supercharged.

Figure 28: Pictographic stone discovered by Mitch Townsend in the Cascade
Mountains of Washington

We tested for unusual magnetic fluctuations and there were none and no radioactivity. Before Mitch left, he allowed each of us to pick three stones for us to keep. But when we tested these stones later, the electromagnetic pulses had vanished and the stones remain inert to this day. How a group of unusual stones could become, for a period of time, powerful radio frequency transmitters is beyond my understanding.

Incidentally, one of the stones I brought home with me turned black and one of the stones Thom Powell's wife chose turned pure white. When I called and asked Mitch about this, he said that happens sometimes.

Figure 29: Alan Megargle taking electromagnetic readings of Mitch Townsend, Tish Paquette and pictographic rocks on Thom Powell's property at Site L6

One other unusual technological event happened while we were on Thom Powell's property. Alan had set up one of his trail cams positioned to record what might show up at the spot where Thom had his possible Bigfoot encounter and where Alan and Tish experienced an extraordinary presence the last night we were there. But when Alan went to retrieve the trail cam, it was in the 'off' position. Alan swears he had turned it on after mounting it on the tree two days before.

Figure 30: Equipment on picnic tables (left) and glow stick inside ball at Site L7, Board Camp Crystal Mine in the Ouachita Mountains of Arkansas

Board Camp Crystal Mine, home of Site L7, in Arkansas' Ouachita Mountains, was the most paranormal active location we investigated. Mine owners, Orval and Cheryl Murphy, told us that in an open space between the Event Site, where the original paranormal light phenomena occurred, and the couples' band stage, some rather unusual paranormal activity occurred on some evenings. As darkness set in, Orval placed a glow stick in a soccer-sized ball and set it in the area. As we watched the glow stick, the mine owners recounted that, at times, some invisible entity moved the ball around.

To invite the possible appearance of this paranormal entity, we arranged to set the REM pod and an independent audio recording device on one of two picnic tables in the open area, then take up positions on the band stage and wait to see what would happen. Nothing happened with the glow stick and the ball.

But as darkness fully set in, suddenly the REM pod went off with the center light rapidly flashing red and the audio signal emitting a loud, annoying high-pitched signal. This action indicated that something invisible to us had entered the radio frequency field the REM pod transmitter was emitting. We were able to film the activity of the two devices from the stage for as long as it lasted. We all agreed what happened appeared to last multiple minutes of continuous activity. We also agreed this was unheard of.

Eventually, the REM pod activity stopped. Later that night when Alan and the cameraman, Paul Lee, went to retrieve the devices they experienced a god-awful sickly smell often reported in conjunction with the appearance of Bigfoot. In addition, to their surprise the fresh batteries in both devices were completely dead. This was particularly odd for the audio recording device since it was capable of continuously recording for multiple days.

Figure 31: Cameraman Paul Lee (left) and Alan Megargle analyzing audio recording at Site L7, Board Camp Crystal Mine in the Ouachita Mountains of Arkansas

The next morning, we gathered to analyze what had been recorded on the audio device. What follows is the conversation between Paul and Alan as they listened to the audio playback.

Paul: "I hear them ... REM pod beeping and beeping away, so does that mean that something went by it versus something being there?"

Alan: "Something is right there, for it to just keep going, it's like it's just sitting there."

Paul: "Alan, it sounds like the cadence of the beeping almost skipped. It's not totally continuous." The two men listened a little longer to the audio. "Now it's continuous, there it skipped."

Alan: "Wow, that little skip validates that something is moving right there, something is moving around right by the REM pod."

Paul: "That correlates with the way we saw the lights blinking."

According to the video and audio that captured the anomaly, the entire event lasted for a little over three and a half minutes.

On the second night of our investigation at the Board Crystal Mine's Event Site, another unusual incident occurred. With two cameras rolling, the members of the team all heard not one but two wood knocks. Wood knocks are the sound of something banging a heavy stick against a sizable tree. In fact, wood knocks are the most common form of reported interactions with Bigfoot.

However, once we returned to our studio and looked at the footage, we could see and hear the team members talking about the wood knocks, pointing to the direction from which they came, but to our surprise, no wood knocks were recorded on the audio portion of our video. Using the most sophisticated audio tools available at our studio, we could not detect even the faintest indication of a wood knock type of sound. This event was most perplexing to our audio engineer, who heard the wood knocks. This event is a reversal of what normally happens during filming—a ghost image is recorded on a photograph or video but was not seen nor heard by the participants.

Site L9, just outside of Elkhorn, Wisconsin, was the place of the last anomalous technological event we recorded. It occurred while the team searched for evidence of the Beast of Bray Road.

After having heard and felt something moving around at what we called the Sweet Spot along the north fence line of Lee Hampel's property, the team started walking to the west when Alan noticed that his camera had frozen. It was stuck in record mode but not recording. No matter how hard he tried to shut the camera down, it would not turn off. Finally, out of desperation, he did what instructions told him never to do. He pulled the battery. Fortunately, the camera worked flawlessly after that. His experience begs the question: Is it possible he was about to film something paranormal and that something prevented him from filming? We'll never know.

The peculiar connection between the paranormal and technology is only now coming to the forefront of scientific inquiry. Unless one is willing to accept the possibility of an all-powerful, God-like being messing with human technology, it seems equally plausible that the many incidences of anomalous technological disruptions could be the result of alien technology interacting with our devices.

Recently, among 21st-century scientists and researchers is the growing acceptance that something fundamental is missing from modern physics, something more fundamental than quantum mechanics and relativity. These men and women hypothesize that fundamental principles or laws must exist that can account for life, intelligence, consciousness, and humans' co-evolution with technology.

Figure 33: Jay Bachochin tries to help Alan Megargle turn off his camera at Site L9, Lee Hampel's farm in southeastern Wisconsin

This idea of a connection between life, consciousness, technology and the paranormal is not new. Since the 19th century's Industrial Age, scientists and psychologists have pursued this connection. In 1884, psychologist William James founded the American Society for Psychical Research dedicated to investigating paranormal phenomena, including ghosts, Psychoanalyst Carl Jung, a notable champion of the paranormal, established the concept of synchronicity—coincidences that are not really coincidences—that he was certain showed the existence of a hidden reality that had a purposeful and far-reaching meaning for our lives. His early mentor, Sigmund Freud, believed in telepathy, stating in his 1922 paper *Dreams and Telepathy*, 'Sleep creates favorable conditions for telepathy.'

In the 20th century's Atomic Age, the famous physicist Wolfgang Pauli accepted the idea that the paranormal world influenced his dreams. Physicist Freeman Dyson, the creator of the Dyson Sphere, wrote, 'Paranormal phenomena are real but lie outside the limits of science.' And Alan Turing, the father of the modern computer revolution, had a most profound statement about paranormal phenomena. Writing about telepathy and telekinesis, Turing stated that they 'seem to deny all our usual scientific ideas. How we should like to discredit them! Unfortunately, the statistical evidence, at least for telepathy, is overwhelming. It is very difficult to rearrange one's ideas so as to fit these new facts in. Once one has accepted them, it does not seem a very big step to believe in ghosts and bogies. The idea that our bodies move simply according to the known laws of physics, together with some others not yet discovered but somewhat similar, would be one of the first to go.'

Now that humanity is firmly in the Information Age, scientists, computer experts and philosophers all concur that technology is basically long chains of information and instructions, neither of which occurs in the physical domain. There is now a growing consensus that information will turn out to be the missing piece of physics. If so, it brings science into the invisible non-physical realm of the paranormal and mystical experiences.

9

OPENING A PORTAL

The story behind Site L3 is different from our other investigations because instead of exploring someone else's hotspot for technological anomalies, Bigfoot sightings, alien contact experiences, UFOs and portals, we used our own property in the Colorado Rockies in an attempt to create a doorway to 'the other side.

Over a period of two years, we worked to establish a portal, not only to see if it could be done but to observe anything that came through from whatever dimension the portal might be connected to. Curiously, once our experiment concluded, as we looked back upon the twenty-two months our research took, just as in the chapter on channeling describing the origin of the Sasquatch Outpost, it appeared as if we had been guided every step of the way by some unseen force or forces to show the world what people thought to be impossible was indeed possible.

The journey began in the late 1980s when my family purchased one of a number of forty-acre sections of land bordering Rocky Mountain National Park. We affectionately named it 'The Land' and established an austere base camp with a primitive teepee shelter from which to explore the surrounding area's remarkable ecosystem.

In Colorado, the eastern side of the continental divide drains through a network of creeks, streams and small rivers that plunge thousands of feet to join the Platte River and continue on an epic journey across the plains to the Mississippi and eventually the Gulf of Mexico. This vast system of glacier and river-cut valleys provide access to the Rocky Mountains' majestic snow-covered peaks.

Our section of land is located in a valley created by the Little Thompson River. At the turn of the 20th-century, entrepreneurs built a stagecoach route along the Little Thompson to ferry tourists from Denver and points east to Estes Park, a gateway city to Rocky Mountain National Park. For a short period of time, pioneers attempted to farm in the valleys along the rutted and rocky path named Pole Hill Road. The stagecoach thoroughfare was quickly abandoned when real roads were constructed along the valleys on either side of the Little Thompson, making travel to Rocky Mountain National Park easier and less treacherous.

Years passed and the homesteads failed. Decades later, a realtor snatched up the abandoned properties. Dividing the farms into forty-acre sections, he sold to about thirty individuals.

The combined parcels, comprising nearly two square miles of mountain wilderness, lie within the Roosevelt National Forest and are part of the greater Rocky Mountain National Park ecosystem. The ecosystem is filled with wildlife, ranging from the smallest of rodents to the largest of predators, including bears and mountain lions.

Site L3, 'The Land,' rests on the ecological transition zone between ponderosa pine and Colorado blue spruce and Douglas fir biomes. The owners of the thirty or so properties formed a small homeowner's group, which worked to isolate the properties from the public by heavily gating the entranceways on both ends of the abandoned stagecoach road.

In the second decade of the 21st century, when I started doing the series *Chasing Bigfoot* for Mill Creek Entertainment, I told a few of the Bigfoot researchers and investigators I interviewed about my family's parcel of land. Every person I described the area to advised me that 'The Land' was prime Bigfoot country.

On a few occasions when visiting the area, I asked fellow

landowners if they had ever experienced anything like Bigfoot. Surprisingly, a couple of them answered yes. That was the beginning of the journey to open a portal on 'The Land'.

In 2018 my future son-in-law, Alan Megargle, moved to Colorado. At that point in time, Alan, an experienced Bigfoot researcher, firmly believed the elusive beast to be the same animal as described by the Pacific Northwest, Salish Indian legends—a large, hairy, apelike creature resembling a yeti[1].

In March of 2019, after a long, harsh winter, we were able to access 'The Land'. Though a considerable melting had occurred, snow still covered the ground. Near the banks of the Little Thompson River, we discovered a single set of prints. Something about their size gave a slight indication they could belong to a Bigfoot.

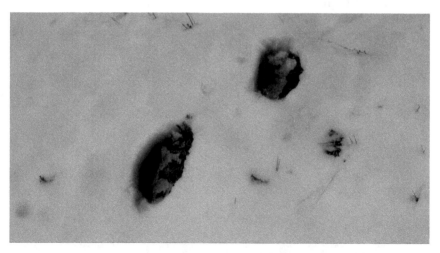

Figure 34: Possible Bigfoot tracks at Site L3, 'The Land' near Rocky
Mountain National Park in Colorado

Because of the partial melting, any real definition to the prints had been lost. Nevertheless, I enthusiastically tracked them in the direction of their origin to a large anthill that had become exposed in the sunlight. Curiously, the prints originated out of nowhere from the anthill. At the same time, Alan followed the prints the other direction for about a hundred yards up a fairly steep slope, where they also disappeared at a skinny tree in a small snow-covered opening in the forest.

This odd coincidence of appearance-disappearance had us wondering if this tantalizing bit of evidence was just enough of a calling card saying, 'I'm here, pay attention.' Whether a benign accident of nature or a clue left behind by a supernatural being, we both concurred this freakish set of tracks merited an exploration into the possibility that something paranormal was present on 'The Land'.

That summer, Alan invited three experienced members from the research organization *Sasquatch Investigations of the Rockies* to look for evidence of Bigfoot and spend a night on our land. Alan showed them four piles of bones arranged in unusual configurations we had discovered by the river. They also noticed some of the typical indicators of Bigfoot presence, such as oddly bent trees.

Figure 35: Largest Bone Pile found along the Little Thompson River at Site L3, 'The Land', near Rocky Mountain National Park in Colorado

During the night, while in their tents, these men heard movement nearby. The next morning, they discovered some of their camping equipment had been moved. All claimed they heard distinct wood knocks, more promising signs for the presence of Bigfoot, though nothing definitive turned up.

Towards the end of 2018, my research had led me to the conclusion that it was highly unlikely Bigfoot was an elusive primate who managed to stay hidden from cell phone cameras as well as modern photo and video equipment through animal stealth. However, I had done enough interviews with Bigfoot contactees that I accepted their experiences as real.

A few of these contactees believed Bigfoot was alien in nature, that is, in some way paraphysical and perhaps even an interdimensional being. This drove me to explore this possibility in the main way I knew how— by making a movie.

By 2019 I was able to secure funding for what would become *The Bigfoot-Alien Connection Revealed*. At the same time, I asked Alan to join me as co-producer. Jesse Morgan, my daughter, Anna, and Paul Lee, my cameraman/editor, made up the rest of the team.

Knowing very little about the UFO/Alien community, I began my research for the film production by attending a UFO convention in January 2019. There, I gathered quite a number of interesting interviews from distinguished people who supported the idea that there was a connection between Bigfoot and something alien. I was off and running.

During the summer of 2019, we traveled to a number of what we now call paranormal hotspots, including one of the long-term original hotspots in Dulce, New Mexico[2]. It was here that we gained a clear picture of places where multiple paranormal phenomena had been occurring regularly for years.

The next place we went was to what turned out to be an amazing paranormal hotspot, Owl Moon Lab. The Owl Moon Lab is located south of Eugene, Oregon. For our investigation, we brought along Thom Powell. I decided to use him as an on-the-spot investigator. This methodology worked so well, it became the model for our future investigations that make up the bulk of this book. This style of filmmaking is known as a *guerrilla vérité*. This gave the production a feeling of the reality on the ground as opposed to the usual partially scripted *vérité* approach used by many of the current paranormal series.

It just so happened that Tobe Johnson, the main investigator at Owl Moon Lab, was putting on a one-day Bigfoot conference in Cottage Grove, Oregon, a few miles from Owl Moon Lab. When we broke for lunch, I spotted an elderly couple sitting a few tables away. Something beyond my normal inquisitiveness as an interviewer for documentaries compelled me to go over and talk to them. Perhaps it was more than the serendipity of being at a conference on Bigfoot affairs guiding me along the path of my investigation into the portals-Bigfoot connection, but the couple turned out to be a goldmine of information, not only for the documentary but my slowly coalescing idea of what Bigfoot truly were.

The couple had traveled from the state of Washington for the conference. They were interested in learning more about paraphysical Bigfoot since they had one on their property. I asked them if we might do an interview for our movie and they reluctantly agreed.

The lady was a sensitive and explained to us she communicated regularly with what she called her Bigfoot. When I asked if she would give some advice on how to do this, she told us in no uncertain terms to turn off the camera. Only after she was certain we were no longer filming did she consent to guide us in the steps necessary to find or open a portal. First, she said, we must create an intention to invite contact using some ritualized procedure when we arrive at our land. Next, she said to use divining rods to guide us to wear a portal might be.

Fortunately, we were able to complete the filming for our movie *The Bigfoot-Alien Connection Revealed* as 2019 came to a close. While working on the edit of the movie, we came up with a plan to try and induce Bigfoot contact and open a portal on our land. Then in early 2020, the pandemic struck. Nevertheless, we decided to go ahead with the portal opening plan since our property is so isolated and we would limit contact to our small family group.

During our visit to the Owl Moon Lab, Alan had purchased a Native American-style drum. The drum was said to have embedded in the rawhide small crystal particles and perhaps a piece of Bigfoot hair. Our arrival ritual at 'The Land' was to create the intention for contact by beating the drum three times, then repeating it three times in succession.

The next step was to create multiple gifting sites. Gifting sites are places where objects are set out in a particular way in hopes of enticing a being to interact with us by manipulating the objects.

Pole Hill Road traverses our land along a rising slope to the north. To the south, 'The Land' drops down to the Little Thompson River, then rises again in a cliff face on the other side. From the road, an overgrown trail leads down a steep slope to an abandoned homestead next to the river.

Figure 36: Alan Megargle and drum at Site L3, 'The Land', near Rocky Mountain National Park in Colorado

Figure 37: Alan Megargle placing a feather in a bottle for the gifting site at
Site L3, 'The Land', near Rocky Mountain National Park in Colorado

The first gifting site was about fifty yards down the trail from the road. We placed a feather in a bottle and set it well beneath a rock overhang. We did a similar gifting with multiple feathers in another bottle halfway down the trail, and finally, we created a third site next to the bone pile. Here we used small objects as gifts and arranged the bones in a particular configuration to see if something might move them.

When we came back during early summer, everything at the gifting sites was as we had left them. So, we decided to use the dowsing rods and ask where a portal was located if there was one. We figured the portal must be somewhere near the bone pile. However, the dowsing rods did not support our hypothesis. They kept pointing to a prominent outcropping of rock across the river. None of us felt inclined to trek across the river and undertake the steep, dangerous climb to the outcrop.

On our third trip to the land that summer, something finally happened. When Alan went to look at the bottle at our first gifting site, the feather was out of the bottle. Alan looked around and there it was, nicely placed standing straight up in a small crevice. Something wanted to play. We were definitely excited.

At this point, just as a reminder, our land is cut off from the rest of the world by two locked reinforced gates. With no way for a vehicle to drive around them, I would say it was virtually impossible for anyone to find the bottle hidden deep within the rock overhang. In any case, in our excitement, Alan decided he would make the trek to the rock outcrop across the river. The brain fog Alan experienced on this hike is described in Chapter 5: 'Sizzled'.

The next step in our attempt to open a portal occurred on November 21, 2020. Alan beat the drum, and as he walked down the trail to the first gifting site, he discovered a mutilated deer. No head. No blood. No guts or organs. And especially significant, no drag marks as might have been made by a bear, mountain lion or human, indicating how the deer carcass might have gotten to our gifting site. It was as if the carcass had been dropped from the sky.[3] We did document the carcass on video, but the mutilation was shocking and upsetting and left all of us in an altered state.

I went off to a secluded spot and sat quietly to do an open-eye meditation. When finished, I closed my eyes and entered into what is known as the hypnagogic state. This is a state between waking and sleeping. I had been playing around with the state for quite a while. It is a state rich in abstract images. Other times people I've never seen before appear, marching through my mind's eye. The thing about the hypnagogic state is that it is like viewing a movie, not like dreams in which one is a player. This particular time when I closed my eyes, an endless parade of creatures passed across my mind's eye. They were big and small and interesting, however, none of them actually fit the Bigfoot paradigm. Some I would call quite scary.

On our way back to Boulder, we decided we should come back the next weekend and do a more thorough investigation of the carcass. We invited Kenny Collins, a well-known Bigfoot investigator who lives in Estes Park, to meet us at the mutilation and gifting site.

Surprisingly, although a week had passed, the carcass was pretty much untouched. Kenny took a pickax and probed the carcass as we filmed. Somewhat unusual was that two of the legs had been snapped by twisting and one other was cut through cleanly if by a bone saw or some other sharp instrument. Alan used his tri-field meter and it registered elevated magnetic fluctuations, though no electromagnetic presence.

Before we left, we mounted a motion-activated trail cam to capture any activity around the carcass. We then decided to return the next weekend to continue our investigation.

Seven days later, the carcass had again remained untouched, which is typical of cases of mutilations. At this time, we were able to verify the high magnetic fluctuations once again. We also determined that radiation levels were high.

After completing our investigation, Alan pulled the SD card from the trail cam and began viewing the footage on his computer. The initial nighttime footage showed a bobcat and fox sniffing around the carcass, though they did not touch it. Then there was a big wow from Alan.

Figure 38: Researcher Kenny Collins (right) helps Alan Megargle investigate the mutilated deer carcass at Site L3, 'The Land', near Rocky Mountain National Park in Colorado

One file captured something I would describe resembling the static people used to see in the early days of analog TV sets. However, this static, which was remarkably similar to the technological anomalies we experienced, as shown in Chapter 8: 'Technology and the Paranormal', is something that should not happen with a digital camera. But perhaps the most interesting aspect of the static-filled footage was that the static articulated a dome shape over the carcass.

The following files displayed clearly defined innocuous daytime images of magpies moving around the carcass. However, the next evening the trail cam once again showed the static image with its characteristic dome shape.

01-04-2015 18:00:23

Figure 39: A single frame of static, dome-shaped image captured by Trail Cam above the mutilated deer carcass at Site L3, 'The Land', near Rocky Mountain National Park in Colorado

Figure 40: Black and white reversal of image 39 (above) captured by Trail
Cam above the mutilated deer carcass at Site L3, 'The Land', near Rocky
Mountain National Park in Colorado

When we got back to the studio, our cameraman and editor, Paul
Lee, was able to clean up the strange footage from the first night and
we could see an indistinct ghostly form moving around the carcass.
However, Paul's efforts with the second night's footage showed the
same dome shape and in the lower corner of the frame, a small
creature, resembling a miniature brontosaurus, moving its long neck
back and forth.

Figure 41: Single frame of long-necked dinosaur-like creature (lower left of frame) captured by Trail Cam at Site L3, 'The Land', near Rocky Mountain National Park in Colorado

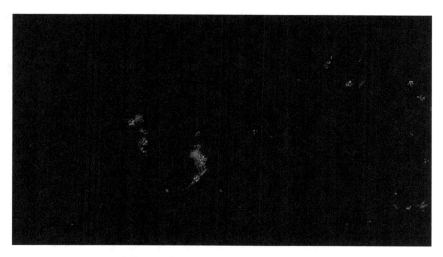

Figure 42: Single frame of unusual creature (center of frame) captured by Trail Cam at Site L3, 'The Land', near Rocky Mountain National Park in Colorado. Note that only the front and rear of the creature are visible in this frame.

Inclement weather and heavy snowfall prevented us from accessing 'The Land's' trail cam for a couple weeks. When we returned, close to the Christmas holidays, we were finally able to map the shape of the magnetic field fluctuation. To our amazement, the magnetic readings corresponded precisely to the dome shape captured on the trail cam's footage.

Once again, back in our studios, when Paul resolved images from the SD card, the camera had once more recorded events, including the unusual static and the dome outline over the carcass. This time, the trail cam captured a different creature moving in and around the carcass—a rather small animal in the form of something that looked to me like a pig-sheep hybrid. Single frames of the creature seemed to show it was never totally there. For example, the front section and the tail end were quite clear, but the middle of the body was missing.

Interestingly, once again, the camera worked flawlessly both day and night, capturing the normal wildlife such as magpies and the bobcat again.

Finally, Colorado's mountain winter weather set in and we were unable to get back to our property until April 2021. By this time, except for a few rib bones, nothing was left of the carcass. All readings had returned to normal. But ironically, there was one beautiful lower leg bone of a deer lying down the trail about twenty feet.

Our filming shifted during the rest of the year to the five-part paranormal series that is the basis of this book. Although, when we did return to the gifting site in early December 2021, we spotted the remains of what might have been another deer carcass.

Had we actually opened a portal and let some unearthly creatures into our world? And had some supernatural force guided us to reveal to the world the impossible? My only regret is that at the time of the presence of the portal, we were not yet familiar enough with using a thermal detector to detect a cold spot, which would have confirmed the existence of a portal.

A final thought on our attempts to open a portal. Supposing everything my team recorded is factual, I posed the following questions to thought leaders in the area of paranormal research. First, I asked them a general inquiry: What does it mean for humanity? Most of these people answered with general comments about the benefits that portals offered, such as interdimensional travel on earth and to distant stars and their habitable worlds. However, when I asked my second and what was perhaps the more important question, these people were understandably taken aback. Since what we did was relatively easy and replicable elsewhere, other people must be attempting to open portals to another dimension just as we did. If so, is it possible that the ability to open portals could be weaponized?

A final postscript to the story of our opening a portal on 'The Land'. In the spring of 2022, we returned after five months. The hot zone that we had measured over the mutilated deer remains had not changed since our previous visit. We decided to take measurements to confirm the anomalous event was over. Like the previous time, we measured no unusual readings over and around the carcass. Alan then decided to place his tri-field meter next to the ground. To our surprise, the device registered strong electromagnetic readings and strong magnetic fluctuations. We confirmed these readings conformed to the original 'hot zone' we had measured last year. Outside of the 'hot zone,' readings were normal. Next, we removed some rocks from inside the 'hot zone' and placed them some distance away, where we confirmed that when touched, their readings were normal. Was it possible that whatever produced the anomalous phenomenon originated from within the ground the whole time? Looking back at the footage, it was clear that when Alan took readings on the deer carcass, they were extremely high. Was he just recording what was emanating from below?

The answers to these questions might never be known. However, the lack of answers, while frustrating, is the true gift of paranormal encounters. Knowing the answers to what causes them is not nearly as important as the impact of the encounter itself on those individuals fortunate enough to experience it.

CONCLUSION

In the 21st century, a new religiosity is emerging in the United States and the rest of the Western world. Named variously in contemporary literature as the Religion of no Religion or Spiritual but not Religious, for the first time in centuries, it places humanity directly in the center of the most fundamental questions of life: "Who am I?", "What is the meaning of life?", "What is the ultimate truth?", and "Is there a God?"

The purpose of our paranormal investigations, as recounted in this book, was to add data to the growth of this movement, to find the patterns in the paranormal experiences of millions of people across the planet in order to show that humans embody something greater than simply existing as independent, socially-conditioned egos.

Indeed, what my team experienced and captured on film fits nicely into the broader picture of this newly emerging religiosity. Our investigations revealed the strength of this growing movement and that this new religiosity is a vehicle for the acceptance of human beings as more than simple animals. It is a means by which all people can see how they are connected to a greater reality or truth.

This movement also posits that while reality is more mysterious than modern science or religion can explain, we should invite and embrace these anomalous experiences in order to learn from them and be transformed by them and use them as a means of connecting us directly with the great mystery of existence.

Interestingly, regarding the many anomalous or impossible events experienced by individuals in our investigations and all across our planet, a paradigm shift of fantastic proportions is occurring. As a species, we are shifting away from trying to rationalize these experiences or finding answers for them to instead asking the fundamental question, "What is the meaning behind these events?"

In order to expand this new reality to a scale that includes all of us living on planet earth, it will have to become acceptable for people to tell their stories relating to their paranormal encounters and glimpses. As humans, we make meaning of our lives by telling stories. The much-vaunted realm of science uses inquiry, research and experiments to tell stories about how the physical world behaves. And historically, religions arise from anomalous events experienced by someone. Stories are told about that event and what it means. And in a few cases, such as Christianity, Judaism, Buddhism and Islam, these stories become codified into a fixed doctrine. As a result, a formal religion is created, telling us the limitations of who we are.

Physicist Brian Greene writes in his book *The Elegant Universe*, "We all love a good story. We all love a tantalizing mystery. We all love the underdog pressing onward against seemingly insurmountable odds. We all, in one form or another, are trying to make sense of the world around us." The patterns that emerged in our investigations are a means to making sense of the mystery Greene eloquently speaks of.

As we noted earlier, on one hand, traditional religions tell us how we are limited creatures, while on the other hand, science takes the human out of the equation and says we are irrelevant to the truth of the universe. It's time to see how special humans are and how we are all connected through a greater reality. It is time to move beyond the old limiting dogmas of science and traditional religions as the only venues holding the keys to the great truths and, while not taking science and religion off the table, give the paranormal and the superhuman equal status in understanding who we are and what we can become.[1]

Finally, using the metaphor of the elephant in the room, the most significant as well as controversial issue surrounding the paranormal is the question: What is the source of paranormal events?

What we know is that these events do not appear to be random; they have a direct connection to the individuals experiencing the events, and each event is unexpected. In other words, a paranormal incident is always a surprise. However, if we were to draw any sustainable conclusion about the source of the paranormal happenings we recorded, it is that the richness of the anomalous events points to possible multiple sources. If this is true, the mystery of our existence and the world we occupy is much greater than any of us can imagine.

THE BIGFOOT ALIEN CONNECTION
REVEALED

See the award-winning documentary that started it all.

The Bigfoot Alien Connection clarifies that we are not alone in the universe. Alien life is here right now, contacting us in the form of Bigfoot, U.F.O.s, orbs, & other inter-dimensional paranormal phenomena. These experiences are changing human nature as we've known it. Learn how researchers have identified locations where portals are opening to reveal many forms of nonhuman intelligence - intelligent lifeforms that are being kept secret.

WATCH IT NOW

AFTERWORD

Go to hangarıpublishing.com to learn more about the Authors and stay up to date with their newest releases.

APPENDICES

Telekinesis, remote viewing, precognition, telepathy, near-death experiences (NDEs), channelings, synchronicity, reincarnation and extrasensory perception (ESP) are scientifically studied and well documented paranormal phenomena. Many of these studies, in addition to being conducted by independent laboratories and universities, were conducted by the governments and militaries of some of the most powerful countries in the world.

Moreover, a growing number of contact experiences from ghosts, to apparitions, to alien encounters, to abductions, to miraculous healings, to inter-dimensional beings, to cryptids, such as Bigfoot, are documented as well. These phenomena are broken down into five categories in the appendices below: Mystical Paranormal Events, Bigfoot Sightings, Unidentified Aerial Phenomena, Unidentified Flying Objects and Famous Terrestrial Cryptids.

Also included in a separate appendix are the devices we used to conduct our paranormal investigations.

APPENDIX A

MYSTICAL PARANORMAL EVENTS

Mystical or religious experiences include universal love, angels, the void, a higher power, visions, erotic union with God, out-of-body experiences, dissolution of the self and a oneness with all, near-death experiences and enlightenment/awakening. Though mysticism mostly refers to the idea of becoming one with God, it also includes the general desire to achieve union with pure consciousness or awareness. Some of the most famous mystics in history are Aleister Crowley, Gurdjieff, Buddha, Confucius, Rumi, Joan of Arc, Lao Tzu, Pythagoras, Thomas Merton and St. Catherine of Sienna.

- In July 2002, the wall of Jerusalem crying 'tears' is believed by some mystics to herald the end of the world. Drops of water flowing from the stone on the famous crying wall are like tears that do not evaporate.

- Islam's founder Muhammad was meditating in a cave on Mount Hira when he saw the Angel Jibril. The angel commanded him to recite the words before him. Muhammad had never been taught to read or write, but he was able to recite the words. In this way, Allah's message was channeled through Muhammad over the next 23 years.

- Our Lady of Fátima is a Catholic title of Mary, mother of God, based on the Marian apparitions reported in 1917 by three shepherd children at the Cova da Iria in Fátima, Portugal. The three children were Lúcia dos Santos and her cousins Francisco and Jacinta Marto.

- In her 1931 book *Experiences Facing Death*, American writer Mary Hunter Austin described her mystical experience this way: 'I must have been between five and six when this experience happened to me. It was a summer morning, and the child I was had walked down through the orchard alone and come out on the brow of a sloping hill where there was grass and a wind blowing and one tall tree reaching into infinite immensities of blueness. Quite suddenly, after a moment of quietness there, earth and sky and tree and wind-blown grass and the child in the midst of them came alive together with a pulsing light of consciousness. There was a wild foxglove at the child's feet and a bee dozing about it, and to this day, I can recall the swift inclusive awareness of each for the whole—I in them and they in me and all of us enclosed in a warm lucent bubble of livingness. I remember the child looking everywhere for the source of this happy wonder, and at last, she questioned—'God?'—because it was the only awesome word she knew. Deep inside, like the murmurous swinging of a bell, she heard the answer, 'God, God...'

APPENDIX B
BIGFOOT SIGHTINGS

Bigfoot sightings and encounters are common in the United States, though most prevalent in the Pacific Northwest, the Rocky Mountains, the Great Lakes Region, the Ohio River Valley and the Appalachian Mountains. The following link is a map of these sightings in the US. https://www.arcgis.com/apps/View/index.html?appid=f987f36187c140aeab6eb157e909eb64.

- 2021 Warehouse 24-hr Gym, Ashland, Ohio – Woman sees Bigfoot after workout
- 2017 Owl Moon Lab, Eugene, Oregon – Darrell Adams documents Bigfoot sightings
- 2010 – Tobe Johnson, Cloaked Bigfoot encounter

APPENDIX C

UNIDENTIFIED AERIAL PHENOMENA

The Unidentified Aerial Phenomena Task Force (UAPTF) is a program within the United States Office of Naval Intelligence used to "standardize collection and reporting" of sightings of unidentified aerial phenomena (UAP), sometimes termed UFOs. UAPs include phenomena such as orbs, colored lights and alien aircraft

- **FLIR video** - The FLIR video was captured in November 2004, off the coast of San Diego, California, by Navy Pilots based on the USS Nimitz. While there is no pilot commentary, the video clearly shows an oblong object tracked by an infrared camera before it accelerates rapidly and moves out of frame.

- **GOFAST video** - The GOFAST video was captured by a U.S. Navy F/A-18 Super Hornet jet associated with the USS Theodore Roosevelt carrier strike group in January 2015.

In the footage, taken by an infrared camera, Navy pilots and weapons systems operators can be heard expressing their amazement at what they are seeing.

- **GIMBAL video** - The GIMBAL video was also captured in January 2015 by another F/A-18 Super Hornet associated with the USS Theodore Roosevelt. The infrared camera footage shows an unusual object flying above the clouds as pilots discuss what they are seeing in the instrument display.

APPENDIX D
UNIDENTIFIED FLYING OBJECTS

An unidentified flying object (UFO) is any perceived aerial phenomenon that cannot be immediately identified or explained. On investigation, most UFOs are identified as known objects or atmospheric phenomena, while a small number remain unexplained. Scientists and skeptic organizations such as the Committee for Skeptical Inquiry have provided prosaic explanations for a large number of claimed UFOs being caused by natural phenomena, human technology, delusions, or hoaxes. Small but vocal groups of "ufologists" favor unconventional hypotheses, some of which go beyond the typical extraterrestrial visitation claims and sometimes form part of new religions. While unusual sightings have been reported in the sky throughout history, UFOs did not achieve their current cultural prominence until the period after World War II, escalating during the Space Age. The 20th century saw studies and investigations into UFO reports conducted by governments (such as Projects Grudge and Sign in the United States and Project Condign in the United Kingdom), as well as by organizations and individuals. Types of UFOs include black triangles, flying saucers, orbs of various sizes and shapes, green fireballs, and mystery airships.

- **1947 - Roswell, New Mexico** - Perhaps the most famous of UFO sighting is the Roswell incident of 1947. This incident gave rise to the conspiracy theory that the U.S. military had reportedly recovered two flying discs, which had crashed in a ranch near Roswell, New Mexico. While this version of events has been debunked on several occasions, some still believe that U.S. authorities covered up the true story of what happened.

- **2006 O'Hare International Airport UFO sighting** - On November 7, 2006, several witnesses, including a dozen United Airlines employees, reported seeing a metallic, saucer-shaped craft hovering over one of the gates at Chicago O'Hare International Airport at around 4:15 p.m. Witnesses said the object was dark gray, measuring around six to 24 feet in diameter, the Chicago Tribune reported. The silent object reportedly appeared just below the clouds before shooting off back into them, leaving behind a circular hole shape. The Federal Aviation Administration refused to investigate the incident, dismissing it as a "weather phenomenon."

APPENDIX E

FAMOUS TERRESTRIAL CRYPTIDS

Name	Other names	Description	Location
Almas	Abnauayu, almasty	Non-human ape	Asia/Caucasus
Barmanou	Big Hairy One	Ape or hominid	Middle East/Asia
Bigfoot	Sasquatch	Ape-like creature	US and Canada
Bukit Timah	Monkey Man	Primate	Singapore
Chupacabra	Goat-sucker	Reptile	Americas,
Michigan Dogman	Dogman	Humanoid dog	Michigan
Minhocão	Big Earthworm	Caecilian	South America
Beast of Bray Road		Doglike Primate	Wisconsin, US
Yeti	Abominable Snowman	Hairy human	Himalayas
Yowie		Hairy human	Australia

https://en.wikipedia.org/wiki/List_of_cryptids

APPENDIX: TOOLS OF THE TRADE

- **REM pod Radiating EM Antenna**

Originally designed as a paranormal ghost hunting piece of equipment, a REM pod is a compact, battery-powered device that has two functions based on the idea that paranormal activity is thought to produce changes in energy and temperature.

The first function is derived from the REM pod's use of a telescopic antenna to produce an independent 360 electromagnetic field. A weak radio frequency transmitter, the REM pod's EM field is easily influenced by materials and objects that conduct electricity. When something enters the radio frequency field, the REM pod alerts the observer by a flashing light and a rapidly repeating sound. We encountered multiple cases when the REM pod detected something entering its field, but no visible object could be seen.

The second function of the REM pod is it detects temperature shifts. For example, a blue light indicates a shift to a colder ambient temperature and a green light indicates a warmer temperature shift.

The triggering of the two functions of the REM pod can occur independently. In the field, we discovered the REM pod to be one of the more reliable indicators of paranormal largely because usually, nothing happens to trigger the REM pod.

- **Spirit Box, Also Known as an EVP Detector**

Similar to the AM/FM scanning mode on a car radio, an Electronic Voice Phenomenon Detector is a relatively small, battery-powered radio receiver that can rapidly and repeatedly scan all available AM or FM signals. This rapid scanning produces a kind of white noise through which, at times, a clear voice or laugh or scream can be heard and recorded, indicating a potential paranormal occurrence. Many ghost investigations have recorded EVPs that appear to be in some unknown language.

- **Thermal Detecting Devices**

Thermal detecting devices, also known as thermal imagers, include infrared thermometers, thermal camera imaging devices and thermal binoculars and monoculars. Special thermal cameras, such as we used, make pictures from heat, not visible light. Heat, also called infrared or thermal energy, is part of the electromagnetic spectrum. Many cameras and human eyes can only detect visible light and won't see thermal energy.

Thermal cameras and other thermal detecting devices capture infrared energy and use the data to create images that can be seen on an output screen or recorded by a camera.

Some thermal detecting devices are designed to display a temperature grid. This can be useful for determining, for example, if cool conditioned air is flowing through a vent. We used a thermal detecting device to identify potential portals. The device would show us an unusual cold anomaly on a screen that we could video. In other cases, the thermal device might indicate the presence of some sort of warmer than normal object not visible to the naked eye.

Also, many thermal cameras have what is called night vision. It is a setting that emits an infrared signal that, in a certain sense, allows you to see in the dark.

- **Gauss Meters**

A Gauss meter is a battery-powered, handheld device that detects and measures the strength of a magnetic field. Fluctuations in Gauss readings in a localized area can indicate the presence of some unseen force.

- **EMF Meters**

Electromagnetic field meters, more commonly known as EMF meters, are handheld devices that detect the presence and strength of electromagnetic fields being transmitted by some source. Natural examples include electrical charges from thunderstorms or the Earth's magnetic field, x-Rays, TV antennas, electrical wiring, and electrical appliances, as well as radio and microwave frequencies. These devices are used practically to detect microwave leakage in household devices.

In our investigations, we used a commercially produced handheld battery-powered TriField Meter. This device incorporated two levels of Gauss readings and an electromagnetic sensor for radio frequencies and microwave emissions. Since magnetism and EM are fundamental forces of nature, anomalous occurrences of their presence are often interpreted as the presence of something paranormal.

- **Radiation Detection Devices**

Formally known as Geiger counters, radiation detection devices measure the intensity of nuclear radiation in a given area. When radiation passes inside a detector, it causes ionization of gas atoms, separating atoms into positive ions and electrons. Separated electrons and positive ions are attracted to the electrodes, causing a current to flow. This is converted into electrical signals, which are then measured as the amount of radiation.

Anomalous radiation readings became part of the UFO experience when elevated radiation readings were recorded after reports of UFO crashes and landing spots. In other words, elevated radiation readings are a residue produced by an alien craft.

NOTES

1. Something's Trying to Get Our Attention

1. A legendary creature in the folklore of parts of the Americas, with its first purported sightings reported in Puerto Rico in 1995. The name comes from the animal's reported vampirism—the *chupacabra* is said to attack and drink the blood of livestock, including goats.
2. Skinwalker Ranch, also known as Sherman Ranch, is a property located on approximately 512 acres southeast of Ballard, Utah, that is the site of paranormal and UFO-related activities. Its name is taken from Navajo legends of skinwalkers, vengeful shaman who have the ability to turn into, possess, or disguise themselves as an animal.

3. Felt Presence

1. The ancient mystery arts began with Socrates and his teachings, which pointed to the well-known quote, "The unexamined life is not worth living." In the present day these ancient mystery arts continue at what are known as mystery schools. There are seven of these schools spread across, Europe, Asia, Africa and North America. Originally these schools put forth carefully crafted teachings to the masses in parables, seeking out those who were willing to look deeper into their soul. The goal of a mystery school was to present the core concepts of universal wisdom, leading to the universal truth 'You are capable of something greater than you ever imagined.'

4. Portals

1. The Skinwalker Ranch sprawls across over 500 acres of northern Utah in a region known as the Uintah Basin. Since the time of Spanish missionaries, the region has been the fount of strange goings on. Journalist George Knapp, an Edward R. Murrow and Peabody Award winner observes that Skinwalker Ranch has "been the site of simply unbelievable paranormal activity. UFOs, Sasquatch, cattle mutilations, psychic manifestations... you name it, residents here have seen it."
2. AATIP was an unpublicized investigatory effort funded by the United States Government to study unidentified flying objects (UFOs) or unexplained aerial phenomena (UAP.) The program was first made public on December 16, 2017.

Notes

6. Bigfoot and UFOs

1. As a result of a private conversation with Bob Gimlin, I'm convinced if the film was a hoax he was not involved with the deception.
2. Rosemary Ellen Guiley (July 8, 1950 - July 18, 2019) was an American writer on topics related to spirituality, the occult, and the paranormal. She is the author of *Atlas of the Mysterious in North America*, *The Encyclopedia of Witches and Witchcraft*, *The Encyclopedia of Angels* and *Harper's Encyclopedia of Mystical & Paranormal Experience*.

7. Communications From the Other Side

1. Most scholars agree that human behavior can, in part, be characterized by using abstract thinking, planning, , music and dance, which have become the underpinnings of prehistoric societies and religion. However, the question remains, did these traits evolve naturally or were they more likely channeled by individuals, or using modern parlance, 'downloaded'.
2. All of these spirit box communications referenced in this book were clearly recorded on video.

8. Technology and the Paranormal

1. According to current anthropological discoveries, early humans, *Australopithecus* and *Homo habilis*, first used tools during the Lower Paleolithic period, 2.6 million years to 1.7 million years ago across much of Africa, South Asia, the Middle East and Europe. Later humans, such as *Homo erectus*, used more sophisticated tools from around 2 million to 500,000 years ago.

9. Opening a portal

1. In Himalayan folklore the Yeti is often described as being a large, bipedal ape-like creature, covered with brown, gray, or white hair. In western popular culture the creature is commonly referred to as the Abominable Snowman.
2. Dulce is a census-designated place in Rio Arriba County, New Mexico, United States. The population was 2,743 at the 2010 census, almost entirely Native American. It is the largest community and tribal headquarters of the Jicarilla Apache Reservation.
3. Soon after a team of investigators for Discovery Channel's series, *Mystery at Blind Frog Ranch* (Season 1, Program 4) began experiencing strange paranormal phenomena, they mysteriously discovered two cases of mutilated deer with their heads missing the same as showed up at Site L3, 'The Land'. Is this just a mere coincidence?

Conclusion

1. Modern scholars and philosophers are re-evaluating philosopher Friedrich Nietzsche's ideas about the *Übermensch*, or superman, in his seminal work *Also Sprach Zarathustra,* and what it means for understanding the concept of being Spiritual but not Religious. Nietzsche considered organized religions to be "nihilistic" and "enemies to a healthy culture." While the Religion of no Religion does not brand modern-day religions as meaningless or unhealthy, it recognizes that religious dogma and science can undermine the fundamental concept of the paranormal, which is, as Lao Tzu wrote 'To know thyself.'

Printed in the USA
CPSIA information can be obtained
at www.ICGtesting.com
LVHW011240111023
760703LV00013B/1131